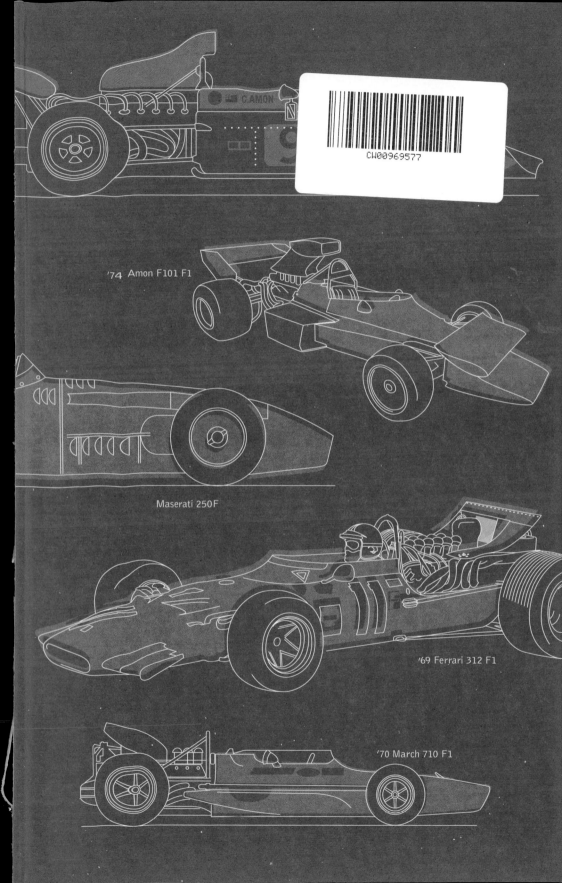

C. AMON

'74 Amon F101 F1

Maserati 250F

'69 Ferrari 312 F1

'70 March 710 F1

FORZA AMON!

FORZA AMON!

A BIOGRAPHY OF CHRIS AMON

EOIN YOUNG

Haynes Publishing

I dedicate this book to my daughter Selina, who writes and illustrates children's books in New Zealand and proves to me on a daily basis that parents can inherit talent from their children

First published in 2003 by HarperCollins New Zealand
First UK and US edition published in September 2003 by Haynes Publishing

A catalogue record for this book is available from the British Library

ISBN 1 84425 016 4

Library of Congress control number 2003104833

Haynes North America Inc., 861 Lawrence Drive, Newbury Park, California 91320, USA.

Haynes Publishing, Sparkford, Yeovil, Somerset BA22 7JJ, UK.
Tel: 01963 442030 Fax: 01963 440001
Int.tel: +44 1963 442030 Fax: +44 1963 440001
E-mail: sales@haynes.co.uk
Website: www.haynes.co.uk

Front cover photo Gary Bramstedt
Other cover photos Grand Prix Photo
Designed by Murray Dewhurst
Printed and bound in Australia

For my partner, Gail Barwood, and my good friend Michael Clark, who persevered and persuaded Chris to open up and talk about himself in the wee small hours of several mornings eased by suitable measures of the tawny liquid. I had my share of these sessions too, but my problem was that I thought I'd heard all the Amon stories before. Gail and Michael were sitting in for the first time with one of their country's legendary sportsmen, and this book profits from their fascination. Chris was an unassuming Kiwi who led the French Matra team and the Italian Ferrari team in Formula One and won the Le Mans 24-hour race for Ford, and all before the days when such achievements would have made him a multimillionaire.

Thanks also to Keir Delaney of Bayonne, New Jersey, who inadvertently provided me with the most difficult words of any book — the title — when he used 'Forza Amon!' as his tag-line in an apparently endless Amon thread on the Nostalgia Forum section of the website magazine Atlas F1.

Foreword

Sir Jackie Stewart, OBE

I was very pleased to be asked by Eoin Young to write the foreword for this book on Chris Amon.

Chris is one of those drivers most people in the northern hemisphere have lost contact with since he retired from the sport and moved back to New Zealand to be a farmer. Chris came from farming stock, and although I am sure he is making a good job of what he is doing now in his world of agriculture, God blessed him with the most amazing talent for driving racing cars. He must have been one of the most skilful and natural drivers ever to grace Formula One. He appeared at an incredibly early age and was immediately spotted by the people that mattered if you wanted to get in at the right end of motor sport in the UK.

Australasia had already produced some great successes, not only drivers but also mechanics and engineers. For me, however, Chris was also one of the nicest people in top-line racing. He had clearly studied Bruce McLaren, who could not have been more mannerly, more gentlemanly and more of an all-round nice guy. Chris was of the same ilk, perhaps a little shyer than Bruce — apart from when pretty girls were around . . .

I drove against Chris Amon on a great many occasions. He was a clean driver. The sort of driver you could rely on not to do the unexpected, and certainly never to behave badly on the track. Chris was racing at a time when track manners were part of an etiquette that was drummed into young drivers when they arrived in Formula One. The regular Grand Prix Drivers' Association meetings, which were only open to invited members of the fraternity, could be very scathing of, and embarrassing for, a driver if he used blocking tactics or otherwise made it difficult to overtake him when being lapped. Some drivers had less mind management than others: there were times when it seemed that when the goggles or visors went down, the lights went out. Not so with Chris Amon — but then he didn't have to behave badly because he was so skilled.

Why Chris never won a Grand Prix is a conundrum that few people who were around at the time will ever fathom. It was nothing to do with his driving abilities. Somehow he never went to the right team at the right time, never chose the right engineers or team managers to drive with or for. He always seemed just a decimal point out. If he had got it right and moved in with the right people, he was the sort of person who would never have left the team. Had he found his niche, a lot of other drivers of that period would have had much more to contend with and certainly would not have won as many races.

Chris never looked as if he was in a hurry when he drove a racing car. He was smooth and delicate with his charge. His technical ability to set a car up was also well known and respected. His mild manner matched his driving style.

We all had great days together when Chris lived in Switzerland. Richard Burton (not the actor) was his fun-loving manager for a while, and also managed Jochen Rindt. Chris, Jochen, Jo Bonnier and I all lived within 10 or 15 minutes of each other. Chris's turnover of truly attractive girls in the little farmhouse that he was renting was impressive to say the least. Richard seemed to be a skilled manager in that area also.

The trips to New Zealand and Australia for the Tasman Championship in the mid to late 1960s were great occasions in the lives of Grand Prix drivers. We travelled as a circus of entrants, drivers, engineers and mechanics, always staying at the same hotels and sharing the same fun and games — and occasionally racing. We would spend four weeks in New Zealand and four weeks in Australia over January and February and a little bit of March. The kind of relationship we all shared then simply doesn't exist in the modern world of Grand Prix racing. Going down to Paraparaumu for barbecues and parties at Chris's parents' beach house before and after the Levin Tasman race was something that wouldn't be understood today. The depth of friendship and feeling we had for our fellow drivers is those days is hard to comprehend now.

Chris Amon was one of the best racing drivers I ever knew or saw in action. I am sorry he lives so far away, as he is exactly the type of person Helen and I would like to see much more of, to chat about old times and, no doubt, talk of new things and happenings.

I have spoken a little of Chris's driving in this foreword, which in a sense is a shame. You hear talk of Fangio and Moss and many other greats over the years, but because Chris didn't win on the Grand Prix circuit, his name may not sit naturally alongside those of some of the other headliners, but my goodness he was talented.

I am one of those people who tend to believe in good luck but not in bad. Misfortune on the racetrack is usually the result of slack preparation, mechanical failure through poor design, human error or bad judgement, but if there was ever a racing driver who truly did have bad luck on a great many occasions, it was Chris Amon.

This book could not have had a better author than Eoin Young. Not only because he is a good writer, but also because he has been a great friend and has been around almost all of Chris's life and times. I am sure readers will enjoy it immensely.

Forza!

The word fizzes with excitement. It could have been coined for the *tifosi*, the Italian racing fans, to cheer on their Ferrari heroes. I asked Formula One writers for their thoughts about it.

Nigel Roebuck: The dictionary translation of *forza* is 'force' or 'strength', but in Italian everyday use it means 'Go! We're behind you!' Fans tend to use it, particularly on banners, with reference to Ferrari rather than individual drivers, but in Gilles' time I do remember scores of '*Forza Villeneuve*' banners at Imola and, particularly, Monza.

Alan Henry: If you're going to call the book *Forza Amon!* it demands the exclamation mark. It means 'Go for it', 'Attaboy' — something of that nature.

Christopher Hilton: From my dictionary: '**forza** — force, strength, might. Come on, try hard! (Sport) Play up! Come on!' I have always associated it with Ferrari and taken it to mean 'Go-go-go Ferrari!' It is pronounced as you'd imagine: 'four-zah', short and sharp, with the fizzy z as in *pizza*.

Mike Lawrence: I guess I could say what *forza* means in a literal sense, but to me it goes far beyond this — it is something indefinable, like the shrug of a Frenchman, the smacking of lips at good food, or getting the eye from a woman. It conveys more, much more, than can be defined. I can imagine saying 'Forza Amon!' or 'Forza Alesi!', whereas I couldn't bring myself to say 'Forza Prost!' or 'Forza Mansell!', even though both Prost and Mansell were very successful with Ferrari — and I admire Prost as one of the few true greats. There are those of whom it is natural to say 'Forza!', and there are those who defy the word. 'Forza!' conveys appreciation of a certain spirit, which Chris had in trumps. You wanted him to do well because he embodied a maverick spirit.

Contents

1 First taste of power: from pick-up truck to Maserati 15

2 A great future dies early: goodbye, Reg Parnell 37

3 High times: the Ditton Road Flyers and 'Big Ed' 57

4 Testing days and movie madness:
   McLaren, 'Aaron' and CanAm 71

5 A dead heat to Ford by 20 metres: high jinks at Le Mans 82

6 Meet Mr Ferrari: the lure of a legend 92

7 Amon black magic: 'I never even won a race' 107

8 From flying start to faltering finish: Ferrari runs out 123

9 Dreams and nightmares: March, Indy and Bruce's death 135

10 French connection: Matra the might have been 151

11 Tecno fiasco: worst to worser 163

12 Amon and Amon: 'I just want to drive' 181

13 Briefly BMW: great to win at last 190

14 Ensign swan song: the end of the road 198

15 In Bulls with the cows: back home but not forgotten 207

Postscript *by Nigel Roebuck* 221

Glossary of New Zealand locations 225

Chris Amon's Formula One Record 230

1

First taste of power: from pick-up truck to Maserati

Bruce McLaren, Denny Hulme and Chris Amon — the three top racing drivers from New Zealand — are always listed and thought of in that order, mainly, I have always thought, in simple keeping with historical seniority. The last-named was the last to leave home to become a Grand Prix driver. If we were to rank the three Kiwis according to talent, however, I reckon the order would be different. For sheer, undiluted, innate ability, for the pure skill of speed, I put Christopher Arthur Amon at the head of the trio.

Bruce was the best combination of racing driver and engineer, but sharper pens than mine have suggested he would have been a better driver if he hadn't been an engineer — and he probably would have been a better engineer if he hadn't been a racing driver. Bruce agreed. Denny Hulme was just Denny. The Bear. Put him in a car and he would race. And win. If he wanted to. Son of a Victoria Cross awardee, Denny achieved the most out of the three with his world-championship title for Brabham in 1967 and his CanAm titles with McLaren, but he lacked Chris's finesse behind the wheel. If Chris was an artist, Denny was an artisan. Which is not to put Denny down, simply to say that he worked at his craft whereas Chris was naturally gifted.

All three were on the scene too soon to be famous at home in New Zealand. They did their racing and winning and fame-making overseas, in Britain and Europe and North America, before television could beam international sport to homes around the world 24/7 and make racing drivers into household names. Bruce McLaren was better known in the

USA and Canada than back in New Zealand. There are few in the younger generation, even among TV-generated motor-sporting enthusiasts, who are aware that today's silver McLaren-Mercedes Formula One cars are named after the New Zealander who formed the original McLaren team in Britain 40 years ago.

Still fewer Kiwis know that in the era immediately preceding televised motor racing, a young New Zealander led the Ferrari team for three summers in the late 1960s, just as Michael Schumacher does today. Chris Amon is probably better known in his home district for his dairy herd and milk yield than his previous life and career as one of the world's finest Grand Prix drivers.

As Stirling Moss carries the mantle of the greatest racing driver never to win the world championship, so Chris Amon goes down in Formula One history as the greatest driver never to win even one world-championship Grand Prix. So near and yet, seemingly, so far. Jochen Rindt, world champion in 1970, considered Amon and three-times title winner Jackie Stewart as his only true rivals. Stewart rated Amon 'indisputably one of the world's foremost drivers'. At the end of the 1968 season, Amon's second as Ferrari team leader, *Autocourse*, the Wisden of motor racing, ranked him as number four behind Stewart, Rindt and Graham Hill, with Hill included probably more as a gesture to his world-championship win that season. In eight of 11 Grands Prix that summer Chris started in the front row. 'If things had gone the other way for me, I could have won the world championship. As it turned out, I never even won a race.' It was the story of his career.

Ferrari's chief engineer, Mauro Forghieri, was a huge fan of the young New Zealand driver. 'As a test driver he was the best I have known, and it's a fact that we never gave him a car worthy of him. As far as I'm concerned he was as good as Jim Clark.'

Chris led the Ferrari team for three seasons, switched to the off-the-shelf budget March-Ford Formula One car for the 1970 season (as did Jackie Stewart and Mario Andretti), and then led the French flagship Matra team for two seasons before miring his career in projects that flattered to deceive.

Formula One journalist, *Autosport* Grand Prix editor and syndicated columnist Nigel Roebuck said of Amon: 'Chris was one of the first Grand Prix drivers I came to know well, and one of comparatively few I would have wanted as a friend even if he had been unconnected with racing.' Amon was the ultimate enigma in Formula One, possessing enormous ability, achieving consummate speed given the right car, but seemingly incapable of being in the right car on the right day. Roebuck reckoned the lack of a Grand Prix win was inevitable given the circumstances: 'Inescapably, by being disorganised (often on a heroic scale), insufficiently disciplined in much of his off-track life and always, apparently, with the wrong team at the wrong time, he ran a good part of the way to meet ill luck. It seemed his cards always came from the bottom of the pack. Even when he was dealing them himself.'

The unusual township name of Bulls comes from James Bulls, who opened a store in the area. Bulls' Store eventually gave its name to the little settlement that grew around it. Midway through the 19th century an adventurous carpenter named Amon decided to leave his home near the English-Scottish border and seek a new life as a farmer in the most remote habitable corner of the planet. He settled in Bulls and built a house on the outskirts of the township on what was once the main road from Wanganui to Wellington. Long before the construction of the bridge over the Rangitikei River, traffic was ferried across the water by a barge operated by a couple named Scott. Bulls is now on State Highway 1, about three hours' drive north of Wellington, and the ferry business has long been redundant, but the barge can still be seen, preserved as a monument to the naming of the tiny settlement of Scott's Ferry, home to the young lad who would one day gain considerable fame as a Grand Prix driver.

Over the years, the Amon farm expanded, and by the time Chris's father, Ngaio, was born in 1915, it had grown to some 1200 acres, a larger-than-average area at a time when farming in New Zealand was pretty much guaranteed to be a profitable exercise. 'Ngaio' — the Maori name for a native coastal tree — is unisex: best-selling thriller writer Dame Ngaio Marsh was of similar age to Amon senior. Ngaio was an only son with two sisters, and, as was the way in those days, he took on the running of the farm when he grew up, initially in conjunction with his father.

In the late 1930s, Ngaio met Betty Fullerton-Smith, one of 11 brothers and sisters from a King Country farming family near Taumarunui. As war clouds gathered over Europe, Ngaio and Betty married. Ngaio joined the air force but was released, along with others from the agrarian sector, to 'keep the farms going'.

Ngaio was an uncommonly good golfer. Not only was he five times a member of the winning Manawatu–Wanganui team in the Freyberg Rosebowl, the top amateur provincial tournament of the day, he was once the leading amateur in New Zealand open golf. Although he wouldn't have realised it at the time, his greatest win was over Bob Charles, against whom he finished seven holes ahead with only six to play. Charles — now Sir Bob — is New Zealand's greatest golfer and one of the best 'lefties' the game has ever seen.

Chris was born on 20 July 1943 in Palmerston North. A drama of the kind not unfamiliar to country folk preceded his arrival in the world. As he himself relates:

There was a big flood in our area at the time and my mother had to be taken through the worst of the floodwaters on a horse and dray before getting into a waiting car for the rest of the journey.

I suppose one of the significant things about my early life was that I was an only child, we lived out in the country at the end of a dead-end road miles from anywhere and, in hindsight, I was really lonely. When I got back from school of an afternoon, I'd have to entertain myself, and this didn't really prepare me to deal with people later in life. I always had dogs, and they have been an ongoing feature in my life. I just loved getting back to my dogs after a race, even up to the end of my career, and I still have a dog.

The Amon farm was within walking distance of the little primary school at Parewanui — typical of dozens of such establishments dotted around rural New Zealand — where Chris arrived in 1948.

I was sent to Huntley boarding school, in Marton, when I was eight-and-a-half, and boarding schools at that age were like concentration camps. It was a real culture shock being sent away from home, and I was very lost and lonely for a while. I absolutely hated it, although with the benefit of hindsight you realise that it was good for you. The problem was that you didn't realise it at the time. I'd had exposure to other kids at the local primary school but to be suddenly sent away from home was something else. I guess it did establish a degree of independence but I looked forward to the three Sundays a term when I got out. Huntley was only a half-hour drive from home but it seemed to me that it was so close and yet so far away in terms of life as an eight-year-old.

Chris was keen on rugby and cricket and recalls being a reasonable short-distance runner.

I was 'knocking on the door' over 100 and 200 yards, but the 440 was my forte because I could almost sprint it. I loved cricket and I always have but I couldn't really play. My bowling wasn't worth a damn, while as a batsman I was probably a bit like Geoffrey Boycott, in the sense that I seemed to have determined how not to get out, but not by playing strokes or scoring runs.

When I came home from school I had a horse I used to ride a bit, but she kept pitching me off. I had my first driving lessons when I was six, from a shepherd who worked on the farm. He was an interesting old guy who had fought at Gallipoli. Dad had a 1937 Ford V8 ute, and I was propped up on pillows and cushions so that I could see out and reach the pedals, being taught by an old chap who didn't have a driver's licence himself. By seven or eight I was sliding around the paddocks. Motor racing hadn't come into my thoughts yet, so part of my after-school entertainment was driving around in the old V8. Driving came naturally to me, and I was driving tractors and finding that I could slide the little Ferguson, especially in a wet paddock.

The last year I was at Huntley one of the kids loaned me an *Australian Modern Motor* magazine that had a report of the 1956 French Grand Prix at Reims, won by Peter Collins in a V8 Lancia Ferrari. I was really fascinated by that report and read it over and over again. Suddenly I had an interest in motor racing. Until then I'd been into flying and had read every Biggles book and books on the Battle of Britain and World War II fighter-pilot biographies. To be an aviator was my boyhood ambition although I don't ever remember saying I wanted to be a top-dressing pilot or a commercial pilot. My long-term interest was now motor racing, but as it turned out I was able to combine the two, one way and another. I'd always been interested in things mechanical.

I had been to car races at Ōhakea, on the airfield, not far from home, but a race meeting at Levin in 1956 was the first since my interest in motor sport had been sparked, and I can still remember seeing Tom Clark in the black Maserati, throwing it all round the place and almost running over the little Cooper 500s. By then I was reading every magazine and book I could find on the history of the sport. I was a real fanatic, and at one time I could have told you who had won every race since the world championship had started, and a lot of the prewar races as well.

From Huntley, Chris moved to Wanganui Collegiate — one of the nation's leading schools, and where most of the boys were farmers' sons. Chris played house rugby at the top of the grade, turning out as a breakaway loose forward because he was so quick.

I was on track to win the 440 yards race at the Collegiate athletics day but I started my final sprint too early and ran out of speed towards the end.

I got my pilot's licence when I was 16, as you could in New Zealand. A friend and I decided we'd like to learn to fly, and as no school pupil had ever done this before, we were setting a bit of a precedent. Our parents agreed, and it was ridiculously cheap. The headmaster also agreed, much to our surprise, so Sundays now meant a four-mile bike ride to the Wanganui airport.

He started with a Piper Cub and then progressed to a Tiger Moth biplane. 'It was great. The Tiger Moth was just magic. I had my first solo after about three or four hours, but then I had to wait until I was 16 to get my licence.' Obtaining his licence at the earliest possible age seemed to be the challenge, and he didn't really start flying again until 1967, when he was driving for Ferrari.

My father bought me an old Volkswagen beetle and that really fired my enthusiasm for competition on four wheels. It was a progression from the old Ford ute. The loose-metal Parewanui Road, from the farm to Bulls, became my Grand Prix training ground and played an important part in my development of car-control skills because the VW was a natural oversteerer on gravel. The Beetle was quite tidy when I got it, but all that speed work in the shingle meant the paintwork was soon well pocked and stone chipped.

I was eight years at boarding school and I'd had enough. I'd decided I was going to be a farmer and I didn't feel that I needed particularly high educational qualifications like University Entrance. That's not to say that you don't have to be educated to be a farmer, it was just that I didn't think *I* needed more education. My parents agreed that if I got School Certificate I would be allowed to leave school, and I managed to pass with top marks in English and history but only about 27 per cent in agriculture. My father said that at least I'd be able to write about farming and to remember my mistakes.

I loved history. I knew all the battles. It just fascinated me. If other things hadn't got in the way, I might well have become a historian. It wasn't so much that I liked English, but I seemed to be quite good at writing essays. My old history teacher, 'Pop' McLean, continued teaching at Collegiate for many years, and at some point in the 1980s he told me that for years after I'd left he'd used my history essays as examples for his classes. He was a tiny chap, a lovely man.

When it came to motor racing, Ngaio and Betty, in the words of their only child, 'weren't super happy about it, but I think my flying lessons may have softened them up'. Chris is in no doubt that his parents were proud of his achievements but also 'pretty long-suffering, especially my mother.

I think she worried like hell.' Part of the softening-up process, unplanned as such, took place when Ngaio and Betty's 15-year-old pride and joy arrived home in a Tiger Mother for Sunday lunch.

> I flew over from Wanganui with my flying instructor and landed in one of the paddocks on the farm. The plane had a manual prop that the instructor manned, and when it was time to leave, I sat in the cockpit while he did his bit. Sometimes the impulse spring that was fired by the magneto would jam, and on this day it did just that. The only way to free the spring to get some spark was to thump it with something hard. The instructor spotted a rock, picked it up and used it to smack what must have looked to bystanders like the inner workings of the engine. I can still see the look of horror on my parents' faces as the craft that their only child was piloting was being attacked with a large stone as a means of making it work.
>
> I started work on the farm but was already thinking of ways to go motor racing. I always said that I had my career well planned. In those days it was my ambition to do the national series — just once. Then I would do a season in Australia — just once. And then when Reg Parnell asked me to go to Europe it was to be for just one season and then back to farming. So much for a well-structured and thought-out career. I went to Europe and stayed there for 14 years.

The farm ran sheep and beef cattle as well as a successful stud, with a string of racehorses and brood mares. In 1971, following his season with March-Ford, Chris bought a filly named Marchere, which his father raced on his behalf. The day she won her first big race was the weekend Chris won the Argentine Grand Prix for Matra. Of course, with the legendary Amon luck, this was a nontitle event. After retiring from racing in the late 1970s, Chris took over the farm and converted it to dairy, running 600 cows at its peak, producing a daily total of around 40,000 litres of milk to be tankered away.

With his keen interest in motor-racing history, Chris, as a schoolboy, followed the careers of fellow Kiwis Bruce McLaren and Denny Hulme, who were racing in Europe. He decided to try his hand at the same game, buying an elderly Austin A40 Special — extra special because it had a vintage Bugatti gearbox, although it stripped third gear in prerace tests.

You couldn't go to your local Bugatti dealer for spare parts and there was the odd gearshift pattern to cope with. I'm sure it was beautifully made, but it was impractical and we swapped it for an A40 gearbox to mate with the A40 engine. It was actually a lot better than the Bugatti. I sold the gearbox to a market gardener to put in his potato sorter.

In fact the little special had been built in 1948 and fitted with a Hudson straight-8 Terraplane engine, but when it had passed into the hands of Herb Gilroy he had bought the Type 35 Bugatti gearbox from Ron Roycroft and replaced the Hudson with the more manageable Austin A40 4-cylinder. Gilroy had campaigned the car successfully in North Island hill climbs and races until he had had a bad crash and retired from competition. The special had then been rebuilt by speedway specialist Dave Lichenstein.

It was basically a dirt-track midget with a couple of feet added to its ladder-frame chassis. The A40 engine was bored out to 1400 cc and running on nitro with a 14-to-1 compression ratio. I tried to race it a couple of times but even if a race was as short as 10 minutes, that was still too long — 10 minutes was precisely twice the engine life of that car!

Our testing was done on the Parewanui Road, which by now was partly tar-sealed. We towed the special to the tar seal and did a bit of running up and down. It went like a rocket because it was comparatively low-geared, and it made a helluva noise, incurring the wrath of the local dairy farmers, which I thought was a bit unreasonable at the time. The local constabulary were involved from time to time but they were fairly good about it.

In my first race I only lasted one lap and the magneto failed. It was a big let-down for a 16-year-old racing driver but it was probably a good thing because something else was bound to have fallen off. I used to enter in hill climbs but wheels fell off, stub-axles broke. This usually happened in hairpins, fortunately for me.

We entered into a project with an English guy who had a garage in Bulls and decided we would put in a bigger engine, so every weekend we were trying to fit a 6-cylinder Chrysler in place of the A40. This dragged on for months and we never did finish it, which was probably a blessing in hindsight because it would have been lethal.

By now I'd decided my racing career was going nowhere, but I was earning a bit more money and with Dad's help I bought a 1.5 Cooper with a single-cam Climax motor in it from Duncan MacKenzie. Ron Frost had raced it. My first event was a hill climb but I broke the gearbox casing on the start line and had no idea who to take it to to get it fixed. I had got to know Bruce Harré by then and he suggested taking it to Bruce Wilson, at Hunterville, who was away on his honeymoon. When he got back, our relationship started, which was one of the most significant factors in my whole career. I might have come across mechanics who were as good as Bruce, but I never came across one who was better. He was a mechanic in the true sense of the word, in that he could do engines, gearboxes, chassis — everything. He fixed the gearbox on the Cooper, and in April we headed for Levin for the final race of the 1961 season.

Duncan MacKenzie had bought a 2-litre Cooper and was on pole, and I was beside him on the front row. I was really nervous because it was my first proper race, and I remember looking across at him. He was staring straight ahead, and by the time I was through the first corner he was dead. I actually got away ahead of him so I never saw the accident. He made a bad start and lost control at Cabbage Tree Corner, hit the bank, flipped and was killed.

I realised that the Cooper was really not what I needed because it didn't have a limited slip differential and it was seriously down on power. By chance Lenny Gilbert's 250F Maserati was in [racing driver and car dealer] Tony Shelly's yard, for sale at £1500. My father was good mates with Tony's father, so I asked Tony if he would trade the Cooper. In those days car dealers would trade *anything*. We took the Maserati to Levin and Tony and I did a few laps each in it. I was amazed at the power it had, and we ended up doing a deal. I think it cost £500 and the Cooper to get me into the 250F.

Shelly was six-and-a-half years older than Chris and had started racing with a Cooper in 1958. In 1962 he raced his own Lotus 18/21 in Britain, and his entry in the British Grand Prix, at Aintree, was made by John Dalton, who, coincidentally, would help to finance the Amon Formula One project 12 years later. In the early 1960s, any driver still competing in an old front-engined car was looking to Cooper or Lotus to replace it. In trading his rear-engined Cooper for a front-engined Maserati, Chris was bucking the trend.

It was going to get seriously expensive to run the Maserati because it used to *eat* tyres. Bruce Wilson was working for nothing but we needed to get some sponsorship for fuel and tyres. We came to some sort of arrangement with Dunlop, and talked to BP because my father used their fuel for the farm vehicles. They said they'd never heard of me and weren't interested, so my father said he'd source his farm fuel elsewhere — and they decided to sponsor me. My father was a fairly monosyllabic, but very effective, negotiator.

So we had the major costs covered, and fortunately the car came with a heap of spares, so there was a fighting chance that we wouldn't have to spend on running costs. Bruce stripped the 250F right down and rebuilt it. He'd never seen one, let alone seen inside one, but he produced an ultra-reliable car. 250Fs — especially seven-year-old ones — were not the easiest things to keep running and he did an amazing job on it.

It looked right, it smelt right and it felt right, but it had to be red. One of the first things we did was get rid of the lightish-green colour scheme.

An impression has subsequently been built up in New Zealand and elsewhere of a wealthy farmer's only child who, at the snap of his fingers, was presented with the thoroughbred racing car of his fancy. Nothing could be further from the truth, for while Ngaio provided the hardware, Chris had to pay all the running costs.

The 250F was a true classic Grand Prix car, and the 17-year-old farmer's son soon got to grips with its peculiarities, which included a central accelerator pedal — to the left of the brake instead of to the right. 'You've got to remember that I'd spent a few years of my early youth on the farm driving Model A Fords with a central accelerator, so it wasn't a novelty for me.'

At the Maserati factory they were unable to understand why Stirling Moss made such a fuss about the central accelerator — it had *always* been in the middle, since the four Maserati brothers started making racing cars in 1926, when they adopted the Trident emblem of Bologna as their badge. 'I know Stirling made them move the throttle when he was running his own 250F and when he was driving the works cars, but it never bothered me. It was just second nature.'

Today, Moss remembers the 250F fondly. 'It was faster and more powerful than anything I'd driven before. But what really surprised me was that it was such a *nice* car to drive. The steering was beautifully balanced, with a slight but definite tendency towards oversteer, which was just how I liked it.'

Chris echoes those sentiments. It was his first taste of power, too, and he never forgot it. He certainly found the 1.5-litre Formula One cars he drove on arriving in Europe in 1963 were not what he had expected of Grand Prix racing. Not the ultimate. Not enough power. 'You drove the 250F on the throttle. Very much so. If you came up to a corner and just braked and turned it, it would plough straight ahead. The idea was that you came up, gave it a tweak and stood on the throttle, and you could have the tail at any angle you wanted, just by varying the throttle.'

The 250F with a youthful Amon in a short-sleeved sports shirt at the wheel, 40 years ago, is part of New Zealand motor-racing folklore. Today the 250F is a prized collector's car: in 1960 it was all the teenager could afford. He eventually sold it for £500 — a third of what he'd paid for it. It is still on display in the Southward Motor Museum at Paraparaumu, a few miles from Amon's home.

The car was bought new from the Modena factory in 1954 by the Rubery Owen company, for use as a mobile test bed for the BRM prototypes. 'They painted it green and raced it a few times,' recalls Chris. 'Ken Wharton drove it during 1954 without any success, but Peter Collins took it over in 1955 and won at Silverstone and Crystal Palace. In 1956 Mike Hawthorn drove it to third place in the Argentine Grand Prix at Buenos Aires. At BRM it was fitted with disc brakes.'

BRM engineering chief and team manager Tony Rudd remembers it well:

It was Ken Wharton's idea, to keep his hand in. He also suggested it would be good for the engineers and mechanics. [BRM designer] Peter Berthon would have nothing to do with it. It arrived from the Maserati factory with the oil tank beside the driver in the cockpit. It wasn't a BRM modification. Later cars had the oil tank moved to the tail when the fuel tank capacity was increased. In July/August 1954 we fitted Dunlop disc brakes and wheels with a gearbox-driven servo. The engine arrived with 208 bhp, which we stoked to 238 bhp for the Swiss Grand Prix at Berne, where we would have been fourth but for Wharton giving Mantovani, in a drum-braked Maser, a brake test — which he failed.

The Maserati factory drivers complained that the 'BRM 250F' had better braking and more power than theirs, even though the works engines were running 5 per cent nitro. Our original small fuel tank wouldn't hold enough to use nitro in the races. During the winter we doubled the chassis stiffness, lightened it and stoked the power up to 260 bhp on straight BP 'K' fuel. We reduced the over-steer a bit, and Peter Collins and the Maserati engineers, Bertocchi and Alfieri, all agreed that our car was quicker than the works cars on nitro.

Jack Brabham entered the 250F saga at the dock in Southampton when the car returned from Hawthorn's races in South America. 'It was a major mistake,' he reflects today. 'I blew the engine in the first race and had to send it back to Modena for repairs. It wasn't long before I'd decided that this car was going to be more than I could afford.'

Brabham took the Maserati to New Zealand, selling it to Gavin Quirk, who campaigned it without success and passed it on to Lenny Gilbert, who sold it to Tony Shelly, from whom the young Amon acquired it.

I was looking forward to my first race with the 250F, over country roads at Renwick, in 1962. I was 17 by then and we caught the ferry from Wellington and went across to Picton with all the other competitors. It was actually a big deal for me to meet these drivers like Johnny Mansel who I had only read about. I went out to practise and realised that I was really a passenger. The Maserati was way beyond whatever I'd coped with before, and to make matters worse it started to rain before the start and I was tooling around in midfield. I ended up having a major dice with Morrie Stanton in the Stanton-Corvette. It had a very similar performance to the 250F in a straight line. He had drag slicks on the back and it puzzled me. In those days I thought you got grip from treads, not slicks.

I was totally out of my depth with the car, and at the spring meeting at Levin a fortnight later I was beginning to think that I was never going to get on top of it. The next race was the Grand Prix at Ardmore, and it was the first time I'd been on an open circuit with the 250F. I went out to practise, running with Forrest Cardon in the Lycoming Special, and I was going quicker and quicker and suddenly everything clicked and I started to drift the thing around and it all fell into place. The next day in practice I did the fastest lap that a 250F had ever done around there, but I suppose the tyres had a lot to do with that. Suddenly I was completely at home with it.

At this time Chris didn't have any ambitions as regards Formula One.

'We had a very high standard here with a lot of quite exciting and fairly young cars. Being on the same grid as guys like Ross and Syd Jensen meant as much to me as lining up against Moss and Brabham later on.'

The New Zealand Grand Prix, run in pouring rain on the Ardmore airfield circuit, near Auckland, was won with classic ease by Moss. Chris finished 11th, a lap down, but in awe of the track company he was keeping. 'I had raced against Stirling. Well, I was in the same race as Stirling. I didn't see an awful lot of him. He was in a Cooper-Climax and I was in the old 250F, slithering around in the rain. At one point I got into a huge slide and a second later he comes past, with a wave of thanks. He thought I'd moved over for him.'

The headline writer in the long-gone Auckland Saturday sports paper the *Eight O'Clock* captured the scene and the man in two words: 'BOSS MOSS!'

New Zealand motoring writer and broadcaster Allan Dick, based in Dunedin, wrote:

I had no money in those days and a trip to Auckland from Dunedin might as well have been a trip to the moon. I listened to that very wet race on the radio and scoffed when I heard the announcer marvel at the ability of Stirling Moss to lap everyone, showing masterful car control as he won the race, but then brush aside the efforts of an 18-year-old lad driving a 250F Maserati as he came home second resident New Zealander because the car had disc brakes, which would have *made it easier to drive in the wet conditions.*

Chris won his heat at Levin, his local track, where he had first raced the A40 Special, but he had problems and didn't start in the final. The legendary Amon bad luck began early.

On the fast open Wigram airfield circuit, at Christchurch, he was 11th again, with Moss once more the winner. Among the spectators was someone who noted his name and was to have a profound effect on his career. Reg Parnell was in New Zealand managing his Yeoman Credit team of Coopers for John Surtees and Roy Salvadori, and he had observed Amon's natural control of the 250F in the rain at Ardmore and Levin. What he saw in the dry at Wigram confirmed his opinion. As Chris recalls: 'Reg never told me but he told a lot of people that he'd never seen a 250F driven like that since the days of Fangio. At Wigram I was ahead of Pat Hoare's Ferrari and up behind Angus Hyslop in the Cooper, and I suppose I was trying to emulate Fangio, four-wheel-drifting through that fast open left-hander before the pits. I *loved* doing that.'

The 250F had all the habits of a pedigree Italian racing machine. *Motor Sport* journalist Denis Jenkinson used to say you could always recognise a 250F pit by the leaked oil. 'It really was shocking,' Chris remembers.

Particularly the rear main bearing seal, which *never* sealed. You got a shower of oil in the cockpit for the whole race — not in big quantities, but by the end of a race the floor was actually swimming in it. It used to get on the pedals, too, which got a bit interesting at times. The heat in the cockpit was phenomenal. From memory, the oil used to run at 110°C and the tank was right beside you, so you had your own built-in heating system. When I was really in a hurry, I would rev it to about 7500 rpm, but normally I ran it up to 7200 rpm, although I know the factory ran them up to a bit over 8000 rpm. We didn't break a lot of con rods but the engines were renowned for it and of course spares were so hard to get then. The ridiculous thing is that now you can buy all these good bits for them and they're a helluva lot better than they were originally.

Allan Dick again:

I went to Wigram that year taking most of the day to drive to Christchurch in a Fiat 500. I sat in the spectator area on the entrance to the fast, sweeping right-hander that led into the back straight. This was the famous Bombay Bend — the bravest drivers took it flat out. The sight of the teenage Amon in the big red Maserati drifting around Bombay on opposite lock with his foot right up it is something I shall never forget.

Even as a youngster, Chris Amon showed unforgettable talent.

A week later, on a grey cold day in Dunedin, came the national race on a circuit of city streets closed off for the weekend. Favourite to win was the tall, distinguished garage owner Pat Hoare, who enjoyed a special, if mysterious, relationship with Enzo Ferrari and was supplied with bespoke single-seaters — on this occasion a Grand Prix chassis fitted with a 3-litre V12 *Testa Rossa* sports-car engine to provide power with a measure of reliability.

Allan Dick, this time at his home circuit, saw his young hero close up for the first time. 'He was suffering from a bout of flu and was walking around the pits — looking younger than he was, if that was possible — wrapped in a grey army blanket to keep dry and warm.'

Dick was spectating on the far side of the circuit from the pit area when the race exploded in a crescendo of noise that bounced off the buildings.

The noise got louder and louder, and suddenly a red blur stormed into view. It was front-engined, with a long nose. Hoare was out in front already. Or was he? A clear 100 yards later another red blur appeared — the Ferrari with the tall figure of Pat Hoare at the wheel. Then who was leading? It could only be Chris Amon. And it was. By the end of that first lap his lead was so commanding that he might as well have been in a race by himself. But it was a situation that couldn't last. Slowly but surely, Hoare, in the newer and vastly superior Ferrari, reeled him in and then passed him. Then it was the turn of Aucklander Bill Thomasen in the Cooper-Climax that Denis Hulme had driven to win the race the year before. Thomasen was in too big a hurry to get past Amon and the Cooper tangled with the Maserati. Amon's race was run. The Maserati careered head-on into a lamppost with the smaller Cooper tangled in the wheels.

Chris suffered a cut lip but the car was more badly damaged. Hoare went on to win the race, but there was tragedy when the colourful and quick Johnny Mansell suffered fatal injuries after slamming his Centro Sud Cooper-Maserati sideways into a roadside power pole.

Chris finds it difficult to relate the 250F and his inherent teenage talent to the competition of the day since he was in effect racing between the eras of front-engined and rear-engined cars.

It's very hard to know how the car would have been back then. I raced against two or three other 250Fs of varying vintages out there. Mine was chassis number 1509 — the ninth built, in 1954, the first year of production. Even in 1961 it was still capable of footing it with a 2-litre or even a 2.2-litre Cooper, but it couldn't with a 2.5-litre Cooper because it got left behind on power. Its handling at speed round a corner was probably as good as a Cooper's.

The observation is personal, of course. Outside observers might consider Amon's own ability to be what bridged the handling gap between the front-engined 250F and the later, lighter and more powerful rear-engined Coopers.

Chris's final race in the 250F, when he finished second to Angus

Hyslop's Cooper in the Renwick road event, was probably his best. The car had served its purpose and launched the teenager on his career.

It had also helped earn Chris an unusual place in racing history: the only driver ever to race a Ferrari and a Maserati Grand Prix car on the same day. It was still being repaired after the Dunedin crash and it looked as though it would arrive late for the two-heat event on the Ohakea airfield circuit.

Bob Smith offered me his Super-Squalo Ferrari in practice. I had always known the Squalo as a gross understeerer but this one had Avons on the front and Continentals on the back and it was the biggest oversteerer I'd ever driven. I don't think Bob had ever stuck his boot in it, because he used to drive around blowing smoke, but I got on with it and was six or seven seconds faster than he had ever been. He offered me the car for the first heat and I had quite a race with Pat Hoare in the V12 Ferrari. In a straight line the Squalo wasn't a lot slower than Pat's car, and if the Squalo had had any brakes I would probably have got past him. I had one go at it but I was halfway down the escape road before I got it stopped. That race with the Squalo convinced me that I wasn't just a 250F person — I could get into something else and make it go too.

The 250F arrived for the race in the afternoon but it was only running on one magneto and I ended up putting a rod through the side and that was the end of my season.

In July 2000, Chris, then 57, was reunited with the 250F in the Southward museum, and it was as if he was meeting an old friend. He climbed into the cockpit from the left-hand side of the car, over the guard for the dual drainpipe-sized exhausts. Why did he do that? Wasn't it easier to come in over the other side without risking the discomfort of the hot exhaust in pit-lane conditions? 'I've never really thought about it,' he said. 'It's just something I always did.' Then he thought about it some more. 'I suppose I was taught from a very early age that you always mounted a horse from the left-hand side, and old habits died hard.'

2 A great future dies early: goodbye, Reg Parnell

Huntley garage owner Bruce Wilson remembers coming back from honey-moon in March 1960 to find the little old single-cam Cooper that had once belonged to Ron Frost sitting in his workshop. He asked his mechanic what the racer was doing in a garage that specialised in the servicing of local farmers' cars and pick-ups. 'They told me it belonged to Chris Amon, and I asked who he was,' came the reply. 'They told me he was from Bulls and wanted me to fix the gearbox, which had been blown up in a local hill climb. We mended the gearbox and went off with Chris to Levin, where he picked up a couple of third places, racing against Tony Shelly's Lotus and Angus Hyslop's Cooper.'

The Cooper was soon replaced by the 250F Maserati, and Wilson found himself co-opted into the Amon racing team, such as it was.

We completely stripped and rebuilt the 250F. Everyone criticised it as being unreliable but the only time it didn't finish was when Chris tangled with Thomasen's Cooper in Dunedin at the end of the season.

Chris's performance in the 250F in the wet Grand Prix at Ardmore opened a few eyes. He had only raced a handful of times and here he was racing against the internationals. David McKay spun out in the wet and had time to recognise Chris's potential. We got invited over to Australia to race David's old leaf-spring Cooper, which was actually the same Cooper that Bruce McLaren had driven to win the 1959 US Grand Prix at Sebring. McKay called it

'The Old Nail'. In his first race, Chris ran over some debris on the track and pulled into the pits to get checked out. The fact that he had bothered to come in instead of pressing on as a young guy might have been expected to do impressed McKay. Chris negotiated a deal with David and brought the little Cooper back to New Zealand.

History overtook itself when McKay crashed the 2.5-litre low-line Cooper, famously spinning out at Warwick Farm and demolishing a circuit dunny. Chris remembers the incident well: 'I'll never forget driving past and seeing David coming out the door of the toilets with his helmet under his arm.' This was the Cooper that Bruce McLaren had raced for Tommy Atkins in the 1962 Tasman Series. Chris decided to buy it, bent as it was, and put his engine in it.

Wilson goes on: 'We got it over here and Ron Frost straightened the chassis and did the panel work. It arrived with us on Christmas Eve and we changed the engine and box from the old leaf-springer to the low-line and then it was off to a race at Tauranga, where Chris finished second to Tony Shelly's Lotus.'

In the 1963 New Zealand Grand Prix, the first time the event was held on the Pukekohe circuit, Chris was running in the first six when he made the first of a series of pit stops with ignition problems. He was eventually classified seventh and last. More ignition problems dropped him from the races at Levin and Wigram, while a broken gearbox pitted him at Teretonga. There were races in Australia with McKay's team but the season with the Scuderia Veloce Cooper was a disappointment. However, Chris had already made his mark with the Maserati.

Wilson has fond memories of those Maserati days.

I was 30 when I started working on Chris's racing cars and he was

18. People have said that he started with a silver spoon in his mouth but that's nonsense. We were virtually a couple of country boys. We never had any money back then and it was always a mate's rates deal, but we had a lot of fun. It was quite amazing that a young bloke like Chris could step into a demanding car like the 250F and compete at a reasonable level with the top international drivers. There was no such thing as a racing budget and we had to scratch around to do it, but I got huge satisfaction from the 250F and Chris's ability to be easy on the machinery. We finished all the races we did together. That Maserati made me and it made Chris.'

Reg Parnell had been quietly working away on Chris's behalf and by April 1963 had put together a deal that would see the young Amon into Formula One. Reg ran a haulage business and a pig farm near Derby and had started racing in the 1930s with an MG-based special. He had a reputation as something of a wild driver and had lost his licence after being blamed for causing an accident on the Brooklands banking. After the war he won the 1947 Swedish Winter Race, on a frozen lake, in an ERA fitted with twin rear wheels. The temperature during the race was 15–20°C below zero, and there was a high wind with occasional snow flurries. By 1948 Reg had graduated to a Maserati and won the British Racing Drivers' Club (BRDC) Gold Star.

Alfa Romeo signed Reg to drive a fourth car in the 1950 Grand Prix of Europe at Silverstone, where he finished third. He then signed with the Aston Martin sports-car team and stayed with them for years, eventually becoming team manager. He gave British Racing Motors (BRM) its first wins at Goodwood with the fractious V16, and also raced the 4.5-litre 'Thinwall Special' Ferrari. He won the 1957 New Zealand Grand Prix in a Ferrari and only retired from driving aged 45.

As Chris recalls: 'I received a telegram from Reg at the farm telling me to be in England by Easter. That was 10 days away, but fortunately I'd had the foresight to get a passport.'

In fact the telegram read: SHELL CONTRACT FINALISED SUGGEST YOU FLY ENGLAND SOONEST POSSIBLE YOUR EXPENSE STOP WE OFFER 25% ALL STARTING PRIZE AND BONUS MONIES STOP BRING LETTER AUTHORITY FROM FATHER PARNELL.

On 9 April there was another telegram: CONCERNED LATE ARRIVAL CHRIS STOP PRACTICE EARLY SATURDAY MORNING PARNELL.

Chris's tender age was raising other problems, and Reg asked Ngaio Amon for a letter of indemnity for the Royal Automobile Club (RAC). A contract was written up and signed on 15 April 'Between REGINALD PARNELL trading as REG PARNELL (RACING) of National Works, Bath Road, Hounslow, Middlesex (hereinafter called 'The Team'), of the first part, NGAIO HENRY WINKS AMON of Bulls, New Zealand (hereinafter called 'the Father'), of the second part, and CHRISTOPHER ARTHUR AMON (hereinafter called 'the Driver'), of the third part.' This stated that Chris would be paid £50 immediately, 25 per cent of all 'starting payments' and trade bonuses, and 22½ per cent of all prize monies. The team would keep all trophies, and 10 per cent would be distributed among the mechanics at the end of the season.

'Mum and Dad took me to Whenuapai, in Auckland, which was our international airport then,' recalls Chris.

I left on a DC7 and flew up to Fiji. It was there that I saw my first jet, a Boeing 707, which would take me on to Los Angeles. I spent six hours there and visited Hollywood. It was another world compared with Bulls. I arrived in London on Good Friday evening and went straight from the airport to the Parnell workshops for a seat fitting in the T4 Lola. This was the first current Formula One car I had ever seen, and I was sitting in it and getting measured for it.

We were down at Goodwood in the Lola at 10 o'clock the next morning and raced it on Easter Monday. It was a real let-down after the Tasman cars. There was no horsepower to speak of, and I really struggled with that. Basically I hated those 1500 cc cars. They didn't have enough power to steer on the throttle. I finished fifth in the race. It was the first Formula One race I'd seen, and I was in it.

Reg was suitably impressed with his young driver and wrote to Ngaio:

Chris arrived safely on Friday afternoon and I am pleased to say that the long journey did not seem to bother him too much. We left for Goodwood early the next morning, and practice began at 10.30am. I was very pleased with Chris's sensible approach to a new car and a new track — conditions were certainly not ideal since we had typical wet Spring weather. There was not a big field for the formula 1 race, but it included a couple of the latest type BRMs, a new Cooper and two Lotus-BRMs. Chris made a good start and he maintained a steady pace throughout the 100-mile event, eventually finishing fifth. His style of driving brought many favourable comments from onlookers.

The next race will be at Aintree on April 27th and I am hoping that we will soon begin some Continental events. Chris seems to be settling down very quickly over here: he has met several New Zealand friends and he seems to be finding his way around London without any difficulty.

Ngaio wrote back on 22 April:

First of all I want to thank you most sincerely for the part you have played in making this opportunity possible. I very much hope your judgement and help is vindicated. We were delighted to learn that he finished fifth at Goodwood. I am hoping that you will impress on Chris the necessity for top physical fitness, which means plenty of training and no cigarettes and beer! I am sure he will do what you say whereas he would argue with us and think we are stuffy old so-and-sos.

Reg replied: 'You may rest assured that I am keeping a careful eye on Chris, particularly with regard to his physical condition. At the moment I am trying gentle persuasion to cut down his smoking, but if this fails, I'll start to issue instructions!'

Chris was replacing the former motorcycle champion John Surtees, who had signed with Ferrari and would win the world championship for the Italian team in 1964.

It had rained a bit before the start of that first race at Goodwood, and Reg had been telling someone about this bright young prospect from New Zealand. They had wattle screens at the Goodwood chicane, and Reg was just saying 'And here he comes now' when I demolished them right in front of him. There was no damage to the car and I kept on going, but his 'bright young prospect' had got it a bit wrong.

Chris finished fifth at Goodwood and sixth in the Aintree nontitle Formula One races. *Motor Racing* magazine noted: 'At both Goodwood and Aintree the young New Zealander Chris Amon showed a consistency and a lack of flamboyance which belies his youth (he is only 19 years of age), and that Reg Parnell has found a useful recruit for his ex-Bowmaker Lola-Climax.'

Reg was a top British Grand Prix racer and team manager who had valuable connections with engine-builders and the racing trade and ran what was, in effect, a Lola number two team. Chris missed a debut at Monaco when pressure was put on Reg to replace his young Kiwi with the veteran Frenchman Maurice Trintignant, who had won on the streets of the principality in 1955 with Ferrari and 1958 with a Rob Walker Cooper. It was a blow to Chris's pride because he was a student of motor-racing history and appreciated the mystique of racing at Monaco. Trintignant had an engine failure in practice and the team had no spare, so Chris had to defer to the French veteran. Reg explained the hard face of racing finance. He said, 'We've got to get the starting money, lad, so you can sit it out and watch this one.' The Monaco organisers had simply made him an offer he couldn't refuse.

On 4 June, Reg wrote again to Ngaio Amon:

I am delighted to be able to tell you that Chris scored his first victory on Sunday last by winning the Midland Trophy Race at Mallory Park for Formula Libre cars. Although this was not really a major race, his success must not be minimised because the car was running very badly. The circuit is a tricky, short track and he was faced by tough opposition from the local boys. He led from start to finish and a second car entered by us finished in second place.

Chris is continuing to make a good name for himself in Europe. It was most unfortunate that, due to engine problems with the car supplied for Maurice Trintignant in the Monaco Grand Prix, we were forced to give Trintignant Chris's car. The reason for this was partly financial and partly the fact that we had offered to loan the French champion a car in order to obtain an invitation for Chris. However, Chris's performance in practice persuaded the representative of the Dutch Grand Prix organisers to offer him an entry for their event on June 23rd. And then Thursday last, I was approached by Ken

Tyrrell, who runs the official Cooper Formula Junior team, and Chris drove for them at Crystal Palace yesterday. He has also been given a drive in the official Rootes works team at Le Mans. If he continues to behave as sensibly as he is at the moment, he cannot fail to make progress.

You may rest assured that I do not show Chris quite how pleased I am with him, since I do not want him to over-estimate his ability! But between you and me, I am convinced that he has a great future ahead of him.

Reg had mentioned a Rootes works drive at Le Mans. This was to have been as a reserve driver for the Sunbeam Alpine team but Chris's entry was refused because the organisers deemed him too inexperienced, despite the fact that he had driven in the Belgian Grand Prix at Spa the previous weekend. Three years later the 'inexperienced' driver would win their 24-hour race.

An American journalist researching a book on the career of Masten Gregory recently told Chris about moves that had taken place at Le Mans without his knowledge when he had been refused permission to race. Gregory won at Le Mans in 1964 in a Ferrari, but in 1963 he tried to persuade the organisers to let Chris join him in the North American Racing Team (NART) Ferrari. 'When the organisers insisted that I lacked experience,' says Chris, 'Masten apparently told them that their stand on experience lacked logic. He pointed out that one of the most experienced drivers who had made the 24-hour race his speciality — Pierre Levegh — had killed 80 people when he had crashed there in 1955.'

Chris had made his Grand Prix debut at Spa, in Belgium, on the long, super-fast original road course that he came to love and where he would eventually hold the Formula One lap record in perpetuity. He was in seventh place, on the tail of Richie Ginther in a works BRM and half a minute clear of Tony Maggs and Jo Bonnier in Coopers, when the Lola oil pressure failed after nine of the 32 laps.

Reg kept Ngaio Amon in touch with his son's progress with a letter on 11 June:

We had extremely bad luck at Spa on Sunday last. Chris managed some very satisfactory times in practice when conditions were good but race day proved a disaster as far as the weather was concerned. It began to rain by the middle of the morning and it never really stopped. The astonishing thing was that Chris, after a good start, proceeded to show most of the boys the way round, and after a very few laps he was in 7th place and a lap later he passed Ginther in the works BRM. Unfortunately his engine had already developed a leak and, as I am sure you know, Chris is very quick to notice any irregularity on the instruments and on the 10th lap he stopped at the pits. Only six of the 22 starters finished the race, which was run in continuous rain, hail, thunder and lightning. Of course we were disappointed with the results of the race, but we were pleased to note that not only the other competitors, but every member of the Press present, noted Chris's performance and were impressed by his driving. We leave for the Dutch Grand Prix at the end of next week and from there we will continue to the French Grand Prix. I hope I shall be able to write to you with news of more success.

Chris himself recalls:

I was very young when I went over to drive in Formula One. I guess I felt a bit like a fish out of water for a while. It wasn't just the fact that I was straight into Formula One, it was also that I was suddenly going to all these countries that I'd read about but never seen. It was a completely new world for me, and I guess in those early stages it was a bit overwhelming.

Ngaio replied to Reg: 'I am sure with his terrific interest in motor racing, coupled with your firm and friendly guidance, he will make a success of it and repay your judgement. We very much hope so.'

Reg continued to keep Ngaio well informed of the season's progress:

Chris drove well at Reims in the French Grand Prix and his seventh place was very creditable. I think this type of extremely high speed racing, with a great deal of slipstreaming, was something entirely new to him, but he had a long exciting battle with two or three other cars for the majority of the race. Weather conditions were far from ideal but he continued to motor fast, despite heavy rain. The second car we ran, driven by Maurice Trintignant, finished in eighth place about a lap behind Chris, so it was a successful day for us.

By the end of this week we shall have taken delivery of a new Coventry Climax short-stroke engine with fuel injection and this will be fitted into the Lola in time for the British Grand Prix at Silverstone on July 20th. Very few of these engines have been made and a great deal of persuasive talking to the Directors of Coventry Climax was needed to obtain delivery, but I can assure you that Chris's performance in all his European races was the deciding factor. Only don't tell him so! He also continues to be most popular with everyone, yet remaining quiet and unassuming. We are well pleased with him.

Chris was seventh again in the British Grand Prix — he celebrated his 20th birthday on the day of the race at Silverstone — and crashed at the Nürburgring and Monza, where he was lucky to escape with broken ribs that cost him several races. He recalls the event in detail:

It was on the second day of practice and it was the first time I'd had competitive power all season. We had started the year running ordinary customer Climax engines, but Reg had a fairly special relationship with Wally Hassan and Harry Spears at Coventry Climax, and they'd come to an arrangement whereby we would get experimental engines. That meant that we mightn't finish some races but we would have good horsepower.

I'd done about three laps when I fell into the trees in the second Lesmo. I just plain lost it and this was before seat belts. I remember going off sideways. The front end hit a tree and the back end hit a tree and I carried on over the side. I was taken to hospital in Monza with broken ribs and a general knocking about and I was the focus of attention for all the other patients when they found out that I was a racing driver.

I was just 20 and feeling a bit lost on my own. I had one night in hospital and then they put me on the plane back to England with the rest of the teams on the Sunday night. Everybody feels sorry for you when you've hurt yourself and they try and cheer you up and make you laugh. And believe me, laughing with broken ribs is no laughing matter . . .

I went from Heathrow to St Thomas's hospital and I was there for *eight* weeks, and for reasons never explained I spent the whole two months in the Accident and Emergency department. In those days they used to strap you up and keep you absolutely still, and I ended up getting a deep vein thrombosis in my leg, so what had started out as reasonably minor turned out to be something major. I would normally have been out of hospital in a week or 10 days but I remember them getting me out of bed to put pressure on my leg and I collapsed. Then I was back in bed and couldn't move for weeks.

One of the big problems Chris faced in those days was actually communicating with his parents.

There was no e-mail or Internet then, and of course the only news that filtered through was that a driver had been killed or badly hurt. I guess it was a case of no news was good news. Looking back I put my mother through hell, but never once did she try to persuade me to give it away and move back to the farm. In that respect my parents were supportive, in so far as it was better to join than be against me.

On 1 October Reg wrote to Ngaio just before leaving for the US and Mexican Grands Prix. He thought there was a chance that Chris might be fit for the race in Mexico on 27 October.

The accident at Monza was most unfortunate, particularly since we seem to have had a run of bad luck up to that time. However, Chris was lucky not to receive worse injuries and before long I am sure he will be completely recovered. We must bear in mind, though, that the story of our racing this year is really quite remarkable. For a virtually unknown driver of 19 to come from New Zealand and in his first season be invited to take part in every World Championship event is an outstanding achievement. Your son has remarkable natural ability and with a little more guidance and careful training, he should achieve great success.

You will certainly find when Chris comes home that he has lost a good deal of weight. He certainly made a firm effort to slim and generally improve his condition. However, it was after his accident that he really lost a lot of weight. I hope you will agree that he has certainly cut down on his smoking but I am afraid that he must make an even greater effort in this direction. I spoke to the specialist who treated Chris in St Thomas's Hospital and he was horrified at the amount he smokes. I am sure that you and Mrs Amon will help us — and Chris — by seeing that he continues with the good work whilst he is at home, and that he comes back to Europe even slimmer, fitter and a non-smoker!

For we certainly do want Chris to come back next season. He has made a good impression over here and a great many people watch his progress with interest. Somehow, though, between us we have got to instil a little more enthusiasm into your son — as soon as he sits in a racing car, I know that he gives of his best and his best is very good. However, I cannot really seem to impress upon him that he must prepare himself better for motor racing. He has taken up squash, which he seems to enjoy, and, as I say, he really has lost a lot of excess weight, but at the same time he still has not achieved a high enough standard of physical fitness. I am sure this is due to a lack of manual work.

When he first arrived in England, seeing that he had little to do during the day, I offered to pay Chris if he would come and work for us at Hounslow but this was not really very successful. Somehow he must find some way to inspire not only his mechanics, but also the people inside motor racing who watch newcomers extremely closely and carefully, that he has the determination to become a first class driver. He must be made to realise that Jimmy Clark, Graham Hill, Jack Brabham and Stirling Moss did not become great drivers just by driving and by having natural ability. Every single top-line driver spends ten times as much time each week preparing them-selves for racing as they do in having a good time, or relaxing.

I think you will find that Chris has grown up during his few months over here and I hope you will approve of the change in him. I am sure that given the right words of advice he will begin to realise what sort of future he could have — but he must learn that he has got to work for it. We will continue to do our best to provide him with a safe and reliable racing car and we will try to produce one which will compete with the best that the opposition places against us. In return, we ask for 100% effort from our drivers, but not only in the driving seat.

In the meantime, I send my very best wishes to you and Mrs Amon. I am sorry we send your son back to you with a few broken bones, but I hope you'll agree that his season in Europe has not really done him a lot of harm!

'I'd only just got out of hospital and I went to Mexico for the Grand Prix,' said Chris, 'but that was a mistake because I still wasn't well. I'd lost nearly three stone in weight.'

On 4 November, Reg wrote to Chris in New Zealand:

I was particularly glad to see you looking so well in Mexico and I think that at last you realise how important it is to be the right weight and in first class condition. I hope that you will take care to keep yourself fit and prepare yourself for an even more strenuous European season. I expect you get thoroughly fed up when I keep on about this, but in your heart you must know that I am right. It will be interesting to see how your experience over here will help you back on home ground.

By the way, I know where I can get hold of one or two more 2.5-litre Climax engines, so if you know of anyone who wants one, let me know. I hope you will take time off eating all that good New

Zealand lamb to write to me soon, giving news of the situation over there.

Chris had heard that Reg had been able to buy two of the latest mono-coque Lotus 25s raced by the works team that season, and wrote to him:

That's wonderful news. If we don't get results next year, it won't be your fault. The 'Sydney Star' with the Lola aboard does not arrive in Wellington until December 30th, the day Jimmy Potton arrives. This is awfully close to Levin so we will have to hope there are no unloading problems with it, otherwise we could be in trouble. I'm glad to say that my bones all seem to have mended and I'm now feeling fitter than I have for the last couple of years; it just shows what a difference losing some weight can make.

I hope very much that you will be coming out for the season yourself; apart from the racing side we could possibly return a little of the wonderful hospitality you have shown to me in England. However, if you are unable to come over we will keep you well posted as to how things are going. I would like to take this opportunity to wish you a very happy Christmas and am looking forward to a successful and happy association with you in the New Year.

It was not to be.

A week later, Chris was writing to Reg again, mentioning that his ribs were still quite painful and his knee was still giving him trouble, although he thought it would just be a matter of time. He bemoaned his financial situation in New Zealand, where he was having problems with the McKay Cooper:

I've just been working out the final cost for last season and running the car in Australia for the past few months, including the purchase price of the car, and I'm roughly six thousand quid down the drain at the present time. I reckon I'll be lucky to get back a third of it.

I've been wondering if you could arrange anything in the way of a sports-car drive for me next year. I think it would be great experience and help financially, which is fairly important as I now have no income here at all and with the possibility of Dad selling the farm shortly, the racing has to pay for itself or I'm in trouble.

I'd like to thank you for the great opportunity you have given me this year and for having enough faith in me to let me loose in such valuable machinery. I only hope I can repay you with some good results next year. I can assure you I will be in the best possible physical condition when I return next year.

Reg replied on 26 November:

I will certainly do my best to think of ways of providing you with more drives next season, and quite understand that you want to increase not only your experience but also your earning capacity. Once the South African race is over, I think everyone will settle down and we should be able to see the pattern for 1964. With regard to formula 1 racing, it looks as though Snetterton on March 14th will be our first race, so let me know when you plan to return to Europe. Obviously we should do some testing before the season commences. By the way, it looks as though I shall be buying those two very special cars, so keep your fingers crossed!

On New Year's Eve, Gillian Harris, the Parnell team secretary who had worked with John Wyer at Aston Martin and would later marry Australian racer Bib Stillwell, wrote to Chris, telling him she was worried about the late arrival of the Lola on the *Sydney Star*:

Actually I haven't mentioned this to Reg yet. He was unwell during the Christmas holiday, apparently spending most of his time in bed, and he is still up in Derby having a thorough check-up. It looks as though it may be a week or two before he comes to the office. There seems to be no point in worrying him about something which he can do nothing about. It is probably just as well that he didn't plan to come to New Zealand.

Chris recalls:

I came out to do the Tasman Series in New Zealand with a Lola but that was a mistake because it was the start of the 1964 Formula One season before I was 100 per cent fit again. The Lola was a real bastard of a car. It was one of the first Lola Formula One cars with a 2.5-litre Climax engine for the first of the Tasman Series with a 2.5-litre maximum capacity. It had a semi-monocoque chassis and it flexed terribly. That car was just *awful*. I never finished a single race.

But there was worse news than that. I'd driven up to the Grand Prix office in Auckland on January 7th and the secretary said, 'Hello. Are you OK? You've heard, haven't you?' Heard what? I didn't know what she was talking about. The news was that Reg had died in Derby. That was quite shattering. It couldn't have been worse.

Chris's Grand Prix career had virtually died with his manager. Reg's team plan had been to buy the works Lotus 25 monocoques for Chris and Mike Hailwood, but to give Chris exclusive use of the experimental Coventry Climax 1.5-litre V8. Jim Clark had won seven Grands Prix and the world championship in 1963, and Chris would be using the same chassis. Reg was the pivotal mover in this combination of special chassis and special engine. Colin Chapman, at Lotus, was extremely grateful for his releasing Jim Clark from his Aston Martin contract to drive for Lotus, and Reg had known Wally Hassan, at Coventry Climax, since prewar days, when he had bought and raced the Barnato-Hassan-Wilkins (BHW) Special that Wally had built.

'It meant that we would have had a car even more competitive than the Lotus works cars,' said Tim Parnell, who took over the team on his father's death. But it was now in reduced circumstances. The various trade people agreed to support it for the coming season but the Coventry Climax arrangement was withdrawn and the team used customer BRM V8 engines.

On 27 January 1964, Tim wrote to Chris:

I would confirm that we want to continue the racing team for at least 12 months. By this I mean that the coming season will determine whether we can carry on or not and I am personally determined that we shall produce results which will be a credit to my father's name. We all know the standards which he set and it is up to each one of us to aim even higher if possible.

I have been to see BP and various other manufacturers and suppliers and I am pleased to say that everyone is anxious to help us as much as possible; however, I had to give personal assurances that you were 100% fit and determined to stay that way in readiness for the season. You see, Chris, these things are difficult to live down, but I know you are willing to maintain your effort for you know how much we are going to rely on you.

We shall look forward to seeing you back in England at the beginning of March. Don't be any later because we really do want to do as much testing as possible, particularly now that we have decided to fit BRM engines in the monocoques. I'm afraid we just could not hope to meet Climax bills in the future and they seem very doubtful about their modifications and plans for this year, so we are going all BRM.

A few days later Gillian Harris wrote to Ngaio, assuring him that Tim was now working all week at Hounslow as his father had done and that they required a new letter of authority because Chris was still under age. 'We have taken delivery of both the Lotus 25 monocoques and the cars have been stripped and completely rebuilt, sprayed in our own racing colours, and they really look wonderful. I know Chris will be delighted when he sees them.'

Towards the end of February Tim was fretting about Chris's return: 'We are anxious to know when you will be arriving in England. We now have the engines, they should be fitted within the next couple of days, and we are just waiting for the first of the gearboxes to be able to finish everything off. Mike is back here, and everything is set for testing during the first week in March.' Chris cabled back that he would be arriving by BOAC on 1 March.

'Tim was on a steep learning curve with a very small budget,' says Chris. 'Mike Hailwood had driven a couple of races for Reg at the end of the 1963 season and he was to drive with me in 1964. I think he was financing half the team with his winnings from motorcycle racing.' Mike was still racing on two wheels as well as trying to break into Formula One.

On 23 March, Tim wrote to Ngaio:

We were delighted to see Chris looking so fit and well and really in good health. Everyone has commented on the way he has lost weight and generally prepared himself for the racing season, and he shows every sign of keeping up the good work. It was a great shame that the first race this year at Snetterton was literally a wash-out, for no one had a chance to do anything except concentrate on staying on the road. Chris did extremely well to finish fifth.

3 High times: the Ditton Road Flyers and 'Big Ed'

'The Ditton Road Flyers' was the title bestowed on the drivers who lived in the first-floor flat of a house in Ditton Road, not far from the Cooper Car Company, in Surbiton, southwest London. Chris Amon, Mike Hailwood, Peter Revson and Bruce Harré were regulars in 1964, with others such as Tony Maggs, Howden Ganley and Bruce Abernethy residing there from time to time. Their parties were legendary.

Mike Hailwood painted his bedroom walls in four wildly different violent primary colours. He was still dividing his huge talent between motorcycles and cars and used to hide wads of foreign currency prize money in his cowboy boots under his bed. Why? Because he figured no burglar would be interested in his boots!

Cooper team driver Tony Maggs was not a serious party animal. On one occasion I came into the lounge and he was sitting watching a Western on television with a pair of cap-gun pistols, firing back at the baddies on the small screen. Normality was a scarce commodity at Ditton Road.

Bruce Abernethy was a former New Zealand speedway champion who had a spell at trying to manage Chris's affairs. His claim to Ditton Road fame was the purchase of the Formula One Cooper that crashed and burned with Phil Hill in the 1964 Austrian Grand Prix. The stripped space-frame chassis of this car stood in the hall at Ditton Road for months, awaiting shipment home to New Zealand.

Chris had ambitions of buying scruffy and therefore cheap 3.4 and 3.8 Jaguar Mark 2 saloons and having an equally scruffy mechanic 'restore' them on the grass verge outside the house. There were occasions when the thus-far well-kept suburban verge looked like an Arthur Daley car yard. The object was to sell the Jaguars at a profit in New Zealand or Australia but the fascination soon faded and the cars disappeared.

When Peter Revson was killed at Kyalami in 1974, Chris remembered their days at Ditton Road a decade before:

> That flat in Surbiton acquired a reputation over the years as being a den of debauchery and whatnot but all — or most — of the stories about it are exaggerated. Sure, we had a lot of parties, but I don't really think we were any different from any other young people of that age and I never partied during the days before a race. Obviously, when you have three blokes of our age in one flat, things are going to be fairly lively. But by and large we weren't as bad as everybody made out — though we certainly weren't dedicated out-and-out professionals either. We used to drink a bit but Peter was never as bad as Mike and me, and even in those days Peter tried really hard to break into big-time racing. He was never the playboy he was made out to be.

Chris, Hailwood and Revson all drove for Parnell Racing under Tim's management. Tim recalls:

> There wasn't a week went by without the police contacting me at the factory about all the drama that was happening at Ditton Road, and the neighbours were complaining that the noise went on throughout the night. It really did seem to be getting serious and I had a few meetings with the police.
>
> I had no problems with the ordinary policemen because I think they were joining in the parties as well, but their inspector was getting rather concerned about it all. This went on the whole year

until Chris and Revvy got drives with other teams.

I didn't dare stay there. You wouldn't have got any sleep at all. I think Revvy shared a room with Bruce Harré, Chris shared with Abernethy and Mike had a room with about 10 girls . . . on a rota system. Oh dear!

In the BRDC clubhouse, at Silverstone, he booms with laughter as he remembers those long-gone rumbustious days, when racing drivers enjoyed themselves off the track as well as on it. 'It really was wonderful. There was no real animosity or drama. The place never actually got raided.'

Bruce Harré, who worked as a racing mechanic and then as a Firestone tyre development engineer, has his memories of the lurid life at Ditton Road:

Our landlady was a Mrs Lewis, who had inherited the house with a sitting tenant. We didn't know that sitting tenants paid very low rent and that Mrs Lewis was actually using us to persuade the tenant to vacate. He had a brass plaque on his door stating 'F. Fletcher Finn — Chartered Accountant'. I had to sign the lease because Chris was under 21. We couldn't actually afford the rent so we brought in Mike Hailwood and Peter Revson. Chris and Mike each had a bedroom and I shared with Peter. When Tony Maggs came over, he slept in the lounge, as did Chris's self-appointed manager, Bruce Abernethy.

We were always getting solicitor's letters complaining about the noise of the parties and lots of other things. Mrs Lewis said to file them in the trash. The first solicitor's letter from a neighbour came soon after we moved in. We all came back from the pub about 10.30 p.m., and it had been snowing. Bruce [McLaren] and Denny [Hulme] had followed us back, and as they got out of their cars a snow fight started. The neighbour on the Brighton Road side was a retired Indian Army officer who drove one of those Rolls-Royces with the headlights about 2-foot in diameter. He pushed his front-room window up and I caught the first of his words of protest — 'I have never seen such a disgusting exhibition in my . . .' — before he was hit fair and square by a Hailwood snowball. I wouldn't have fancied living next door to us.

We met each evening after work at The Gloucester Arms in Kingston-upon-Thames, and we used to say that if Chris wasn't singing *Danny Boy* by 8.00 p.m. it was going to be a quiet evening. Our favourite restaurant was The Contented Plaice nearby, overlooking the Thames, and when Chris booked the complete top floor for his 21st birthday party, all the Grand Prix drivers were there and the piano player was belting out old favourites while everyone joined in the choruses. BP had agreed to fund the party on the understanding that their film crew would be present, shooting footage for a documentary they were making on what their sponsored drivers did between the French Grand Prix and the British. The problem was this didn't seem to have been shared with the camera crew, who joined in the party with gusto — and never shot a foot of film. The BP management were not at all happy, until we offered to stage the party again later in the year — and they agreed. The replay was reckoned to be even better than the original.

The party for Chris's 21st seemed to last most of the week. One night around 11.00 p.m. there was a loud knocking on our floor, which was presumably the ground-floor tenant using a broomstick to vent his anger. I went downstairs with a pretty girl from the party, and when the door opened there was the tenant, F. Fletcher Finn, in his pyjamas and wearing a nightcap. He wasn't quite prepared for this pretty young girl, who said, 'Fuckleberry Finn — f**k off!'

Within a couple of days a furniture truck arrived, Mr F. Fletcher Finn was gone and Mrs Lewis had achieved her objective of renting to these 'two nice boys from New Zealand'. Before I could get our deposit back from Mrs Lewis, I had to retrieve two drawers from the chest in Mike's room — rather than pack suitcases, Mike had just taken the drawers with his clothes in them.

While preparing his 1993 book *Champions of Speed*, on the careers of McLaren, Hulme and Amon, New Zealand author Richard Becht asked Chris about quotes of mine on the parties that had appeared in David Tremayne's *Racers Apart*. Becht wrote:

Amon's version of events is a little milder on his own antics, a bit richer on Young's performance. 'The Gloucester Arms was a great watering hole and we had a lot of fun there, perhaps too much. Being only 20, I was pretty much swept along with anything, albeit some of Eoin's stories are exaggerated in that he sometimes thinks everybody else was doing the drinking and he wasn't.'

For Chris, 1964 was a lost season in Formula One, with a best finish of fifth in the Dutch Grand Prix at Zandvoort and just two points in the world championship. In nontitle races he was fourth in the Mediterranean Grand Prix at Enna and fifth at Snetterton, Syracuse and Silverstone, with the Parnell Lotus-BRM. He remembers the race at Enna:

The circuit went round a lake full of water snakes and it was quick as hell. The cars would only do about 160 mph and we were *averaging* 130–140 mph. On the first lap of the race Mike [Hailwood] got away in front of me and going round this 140 mph corner he lost the whole bloody lot. I ducked round the back and saw this thing in the mirrors launch itself into the lake. The next lap round and Mike was standing on the bank absolutely soaked. We had those Dunlop blue overalls and he was dripping wet. He said he'd got out as fast as he could — remembering the snakes.

Chris's first drive for Carroll Shelby's team was in the Daytona coupé at Le Mans in 1964, where he teamed up with Jochen Neerpasch. 'It was a big-budget operation, a great set-up, and the cars were wonderful to drive. I just loved them, and we were well ahead of the GTO Ferraris in our class at Le Mans. You drove them much like the 250F — all that power and bugger-all traction.'

They led the GT category at Le Mans until they were caught using an illegal battery to jump-start the car during a pit stop and disqualified, but Chris had shown enough talent to be retained for 1965 and 1966, when Shelby ran Ford GT40s.

My second drive in 1965 was in the Nürburgring 1000-kilometre race. I made a good start and was running near the front when I ran out of fuel only a couple of miles from the pits and had to push the car in. There had been a stuff-up with the pit signals and I thought I was due to stop on the following lap. At Le Mans I was teamed with Phil Hill in a long-nosed GT40, and I was happy to be not just on but ahead of Phil's pace.

Then there was a heroic second place to 'Gentleman Jack' Sears at Brands Hatch, the two drivers racing nose to tail and side by side in Cobras. Chris's palms were rubbed raw from fighting the wheel but it was an awesome drive and reminded anyone who needed reminding that the Amon talent was still there. As *Motor Racing* related it:

The battle between Jack Sears and Chris Amon for victory in the GT section went all the way with just 1.4sec separating the Willment and Atkins Shelby American Cobras at the finish. This was a wonderful dice, with the massively built cars drifting very smoothly on their fat Goodyears, Sears seeming to have the edge on steam out of the corners, and Amon closing up on braking. A great dice, from which a dead heat would have been a fitting verdict.

While the bloodied Amon palms made good copy, Chris pointed out later that he had in fact got the blisters that burst during his Herculean drive in the big Cobra during the German Grand Prix on the Nürburgring the same weekend.

As far as Formula One was concerned, Chris's 1965 season was more of a sabbatical thrust upon him, but his summer working with Firestone development engineers stood him in the sort of stead that modern young Formula One men gain when they sign as test driver with a top team. Bruce McLaren had probably taught Chris the fundamentals of testing and development driving, but Chris also had his own natural fingertip flair, which proved invaluable as the American tyre company came to grips with the new — to them — world of Grand Prix racing.

Bruce also arranged for Chris to race a 2-litre Elva-BMW as a sort of sideline to the arrangement whereby Elva built production customer versions of the McLaren CanAm sports racing cars. When wins came for Chris they seemed to come in queues.

The *Grosser Preis der Solitude* for Formula Two was scheduled for the same weekend as the Dutch Grand Prix at Zandvoort, so the top Formula Two teams were chasing drivers. Chris was signed to drive a Lola-Cosworth T60 for the Midland Racing Partnership, with Australian Paul Hawkins in a BRM-powered Lola and American Roy Pike in a 1964 T55 Lola-Cosworth. The Ron Harris works-supported Lotus team brought four cars. Peter Revson was driving the Cosworth-engined Lotus normally raced by Mike Spence, while Brian Hart and German driver Hans Herrmann drove two BRM-engined cars. Alan Rees, Gerhard Mitter and Trevor Taylor were all in Brabhams. The 7.09-mile circuit was damp on the first practice day, Friday, but it teemed on the Saturday, so Friday's times stood for the grid, with Revson on pole at 4 minutes 9.5 seconds, Amon just a tenth of a second slower, and Rees completing the front row of the grid: Lotus, Lola, Brabham.

It was Trevor Taylor who took the lead at the start, bursting through from the second row, and they came past the pits on the first lap in the order Taylor, Revson, Amon, Rees. The leaders changed in the early laps and soon it was Rees and Amon out front, but by lap 4 Amon was leading and Rees was defending his second place against local German driver Mitter. Rees set a new lap record of 4 minutes 1.5 seconds (at an average speed of 105.76 mph) in the Brabham, but Amon was the winner by 9.6 seconds with Mitter a further 3.7 seconds back. Chris had averaged 104.08 mph in the 1000 cc Lola-Cosworth.

The following Saturday Chris was wearing the winner's laurels again, this time in the 5-litre McLaren-Elva sports car at Silverstone, where he whipped the top-class field to take the flag two laps ahead at an average speed of 108.48 mph. This was a faster average than the Formula One cars had set in the British Grand Prix a few weeks earlier.

Chris's sports-car win was a good indication of his improvement over the previous season. Practice dramas had seen the McLaren-Elva catch fire, and Bruce McLaren had been treated for second-degree burns after leaping from the car with his jacket blazing. This was before safety had become fashionable, and Bruce was wearing his green nylon rally jacket with the McLaren Racing Team shield on the pocket. He rolled in the grass and put out the flames, but not before the burning nylon had melted painfully through his overalls. Reserve driver Chris Amon was setting out for dinner

∧
Racing against Moss, McLaren and Surtees at Ardmore in 1962 in the beloved 250F Maserati. Well, in the same race, at least.

>
The original Amon helmet, as seen in Europe, 1963.

∧
Amon's Lola is first in line for practice at the Nürburgring, 1963.

∧
No sunbeams for this Rapier at a damp Brands Hatch in 1963.

NICK LOUDEN

∧
Aboard Ken Tyrell's Formula Junior Cooper.

>
1964, and Chris is a stone lighter after his crash at Monza the previous year.

^
A briefing session with Tim Parnell and Bruce Abernathy at Brands Hatch, 1964.

^
The mother of all dices — chasing Jack Sears in the Guards Trophy, August 1964.

∧
Running the McLaren M1B in a Group 7 race at Snetterton, 1966.

∧
The Ford GT-40 team in the Le Mans pits, 1966. Bruce McLaren and Chris Amon (2) finished first, while Ken Miles and Denny Hulme (1) finished second.

Λ
Chris with Jackie Stewart (centre) and Al Unser (right) at the Indy 500 in 1967.

DAVE FRIEDMAN

Λ
Lorenzo Bandini's number one status ensures he gets pole position with Miss Universe after the
24-hour Daytona Continental.

∧
Chasing AJ Foyt aboard the winning Ford in the 1967 Le Mans 24-hour endurance test.

∧
At Brands Hatch in 1967.

∧
Preparing for the first of two New Zealand Grand Prix victories, Pukekohe, 1968.

∧
En route to second place in the 1968 Lady Wigram Trophy race.

BILL POTTINGER

in London when Bruce phoned him to say he would have to race the following day.

Having missed official practice, Chris had to start from the back of the 35-car grid with his main opponent, John Surtees, on pole position after recording an average 110 mph in his 6-litre Lola. Boeing pilot Hugh Dibley also had a 6-litre Lola, and Australian Frank Gardner had a 4.7-litre Lotus 30. Amon left the line with tyres smoking and had snaked past 12 cars before the first corner. At the end of the second lap he was fourth, behind Surtees, Dibley and Gardner, and a lap later he was up to second place and whittling down the lead that Surtees had opened up before his young rival had cleared the pack.

On the fifth lap Surtees set a new circuit record at 115.54 mph, but the strain told and his 450 bhp Chevvy V8 blew up. With 120 miles of racing left, Amon kept pounding round with the McLaren-Elva never missing a beat as his pursuers dropped behind. Dibley's gearbox split, Gardner's clutch broke and Amon eventually won by two laps from Peter Revson in a little 2-litre Brabham — celebrations back at Ditton Road! — and David Piper in a 250LM Ferrari.

Bruce had been relegated to pit manager while his Kiwi protégé raced out in the lead. As if his burns weren't uncomfortable enough, he was hit by a car speeding into the pits with a door hanging open.

A crash at 120 mph on the Monday after this winning week wrecked the prototype McLaren-Elva test car. Chris was testing Firestone tyres at Brands Hatch when it slewed to the right as he was accelerating hard in fourth gear on the straight. Realising the situation was beyond his control, he dived under the dash panel and received his only injury — a grazed nose — when the car careered bonnet-first into the bank, had its tail smashed in further down the road and glanced off a concrete bridge support that tore off a wheel. He stepped dazed from the broken car to see wreckage scattered for 150 yards up the track. 'It was like a plane crash,' he said afterwards.

A rose joint broke in the rear suspension and the car just turned sharp right into the bank. I ended up sitting in the seat and the rest of the car was scattered up the road.

They had this ancient World War II surplus ambulance, and by the time it had arrived and I was in it, I was going into shock. I remember coming to in hospital and being greeted by two Indian doctors and a couple of Indian nurses. I knew I'd had a big crash, but how could I have ended up in Calcutta?

A few weeks later, Chris drove the big McLaren again to win the sports-car race at Sainte Jovite, in Canada.

He also had a stint at the wheel of a special experimental open version of a Le Mans Ford GT built in secret at the McLaren workshops, financed by Ford as a development project with competition possibilities. It was built by Gary Knutson and Howden Ganley in a walled-off section of the workshop in Feltham, in Middlesex. As Chris tells the story:

I ran it in the CanAm series and it was a bloody disaster. It was too heavy and it didn't have enough horsepower. We called it 'Big Ed' after the Edsel model that had been less than successful. It had the top cut off and a two-speed torque converter and it didn't go worth a damn.

I remember the Ford hierarchy being at Riverside when we were testing and it was *way* off the pace. The Ford people told Bruce that they thought it was the driver — me — and Bruce was *really* irate at that suggestion. They said they wanted Phil Hill to have a few laps — and if they thought it was off the pace with me, it was even *further* off the pace with Phil. But we soldiered on with it and the last race I did in 'Big Ed' was during the Nassau Speed Week, in the Bahamas. Those races were great fun. A guy called Jean Beech had entered Bruce and me in the Formula Vee race, and there were two heats on the Friday with the race on Sunday. There were 80 entries. Bruce wasn't due to arrive until the Saturday and I won my heat on the Friday but I preferred his engine to the one in my car, so I had it switched before he arrived. I told him about it just before the start. I said, 'You know the deal here, Bruce, don't you? I drove your car in the heat on Friday — and I've got your engine and you've got my car.' He roared with laughter and said, 'You bastard!' After the race he wrote to his father and said, 'I think we've taught him too well.'

In the race I disappeared at the start and won while Bruce eventually managed to extricate himself from the grid and finished second. I won $10,000, which was bloody good money in those days but [McLaren director] Teddy Mayer fronted up and demanded half the prize money. I protested that I was driving for Beech, not McLaren, but Teddy said they'd paid my expenses to get there and drive it and the Ford thing. The result was that I lost half my prize money. Still, the parties were good. They had one at a different tourist hotel every night.

Howden Ganley tells a slightly less condemnatory version of the 'Big Ed' saga, and since he was closely involved in the building and racing of the car, his view can be allowed to stand:

The purpose of the X-1 project was to be a test vehicle for Ford. No doubt Christopher had the idea that it would be no more than a Le Mans car with the roof cut off and that he would be competitive with the purpose-built CanAm cars in the series.

When we first completed the car at Feltham, it was fitted with a Hewland LG gearbox and weighed 1920 lbs (with the heavy old Le Mans nose), which was nearly 1000 lbs lighter than the 7-litre Le Mans Fords. It qualified fourth at Mosport and retired in the race, and then we went to Ford's Kar Kraft facility, where we were instructed to fit a Ford 4-speed transmission in place of 'that funny little Limey transaxle'. We also fitted a much lighter nose but the overall effect was that the total weight had been increased.

We then went to Riverside, where Chris says the car was 'a bloody disaster'. According to the Ford development document, 'The 4-speed manual unit performed faultlessly . . . Although the X-1 vehicle is not competitive as a modified racer it is providing us with considerable background to develop the "J" car.'

As a mechanic I was unaware of any Ford unhappiness about Chris's driving. Bruce, Phil Hill and Chris drove the car in the Riverside tests. Phil did 18 laps with a best time of 1 minute 35 seconds. Bruce did 15 laps the next day with a best of 1 minute 34 seconds, and after a couple of days with the car Chris was down to 1 minute 31 seconds. In the race Chris was fifth behind Hap Sharp, with Chaparral, Jim Clark, with Lotus, Bruce, in the McLaren, and Charlie Hayes, also with McLaren.

We then took the car to Nassau, and my recollection is that although it was supposed to have a two-speed automatic transmission, this didn't actually get fitted for that event. We did blow an engine in one of the races, and I remember fitting another, rolling around on the floor of that old wooden hangar where all the cars were stored.

After Nassau we stopped off at Daytona for more testing. I had fitted a big FIA windscreen which had been flown down to Nassau by Ford. I was supposed to adapt this monster on to 'Big Ed' with no equipment, just me and my spanners in the aforementioned hangar. Somehow I managed it, but being given the job was an indication of the sometimes unrealistic expectations of some of the Ford hierarchy.

From Daytona I took the car back to Kar Kraft at Dearborn. I met up with McLaren team manager Teddy Mayer there and he asked me to come back in January to be crew chief on 'Big Ed' in a development programme on automatic transmissions and brakes. We actually had two cars with a variety of transmissions. There were two automatics, one a two-speed version of the four-speed manual but with a fluid flywheel as on the Chaparral, and the other a three-speed full automatic copied off the Ford Fairlane transmission.

After what seemed like years grinding around at Sebring with Ken Miles, Ronnie Bucknum and Chris driving, I was told to take the X-1 to Daytona as a spare car for the 24-hour race. Ken Miles had been very impressed with the X-1 and obviously told Carroll Shelby about it, so they took the car home with them and they went on to win Sebring with it. At the Sebring tests the X-1 was clearly the fastest of all the Fords, helped no doubt by it being lighter and also by the improved brakes.

The net result was that the car probably did what Ford expected of it, considerable funds found their way to McLaren Racing, which was very important at that time — and it was not really the total fiasco that Chris remembers. For me it was a great opportunity to learn a lot about vehicle engineering, and to earn a considerable amount of money to put towards my real aim, which was to revive my own driving career and try to get into Formula One.

Ganley achieved his aim. In 1967 he was in Formula Three with his own Brabham, and in 1970, with encouragement from Bruce McLaren, he was in Formula 5000 with a McLaren M10B entered by Bruce's neighbour,

Barry Newman. In 1971 and 1972 Ganley was a BRM works driver in Formula One, and in 1973 he drove for Williams. He retired from racing after a bad crash when his Japanese Maki suffered suspension failure in the German Grand Prix on the old Nürburgring. Ganley is currently a board member of the prestigious BRDC.

4

Testing days and movie madness: McLaren, 'Aaron' and CanAm

Not all the Amon races followed convention. One less-than-orthodox affair took place when Chris agreed to co-drive Swedish driver Ulf Norrinder's Ferrari GTO in the 12-hour race at Reims in 1965.

> Ulf sent a telegram at the last minute to say that he couldn't make it because he was getting married, so I phoned up this young new Scottish guy, Jackie Stewart. A piston failed in practice and Ulf's Swedish mechanic was all for going home, but I had New Zealander Bruce Harré with me and he scrounged bits from other teams and rebuilt the engine. It was quite incredible, the way Bruce sorted that engine out. In the race we made a stop to change pads and realised that the new pads were locked in the boot of our car in the pits and we couldn't find the keys. Then there was the pit stop to change tyres and we couldn't find the second spare. It took a while before someone thought to look in the boot — and the spare wheel was there.

Bill Gavin, a New Zealand journalist and long-time friend and confidant of Chris Amon, wrote a considered profile in *Speed World International* in August 1968: 'That Chris didn't get a lot of rides in this period was as much his own fault as anybody else's. At the time Chris had a fairly generous income from his father's farm in New Zealand, and lived what seemed a fairly indolent and carefree existence in the Surbiton flat he shared with Mike Hailwood and others of similar bent.'

Chris's ability as a test driver was almost ethereal. A couple of occasions stand out. At a Goodwood test in 1965, with the McLaren pounding round the track alone for lap after lap, Bruce Harré and the Firestone crew decided to alleviate the boredom by playing what they considered a joke on Chris. They took off one set of tyres, shuffled the wheels around, and then put the same tyres back on. The sports-racer rumbled back on to the track to laughter all round. But then they were struck by the implication of what they had done. If Chris did a few laps and came back rating the tyres as better or worse than the previous set when they were, in fact, the same set, his ability as an expert tester would be severely called into question. The laughter was over and they waited nervously for the next stop.

The McLaren cruised down the pit lane and pulled up beside the crew. Chris sat there and said nothing, a puzzled look on his face. 'I don't know how to say this, you guys, but that set feels *exactly* like the set you took off last time.' He never saw the looks of relief on the Firestone faces and didn't hear the story until some time later.

'The tyre-testing was really quite physical because we were doing probably 250 to 300 miles in a day, flat out,' he relates.

I used to drive pretty well right on my limit because you had to, really. The cars were physical, too. They were very heavy in the steering so at the end of the day you certainly knew you'd done a hard day's work.

We did most of our testing at Goodwood, Snetterton and Oulton Park, and we'd be away for two or three days at a time. One of the tyre fitters, Ernie Brawn, used to cook up these steak-and-kidney puddings in the back of the van — real stodge that was guaranteed to add at least a second a lap to the afternoon times. It wasn't until years later that I discovered Ernie's son was Ross

Brawn, technical director and Michael Schumacher's mentor at Ferrari.

Bruce Harré was one of the early Kiwi McLaren mechanics who worked on the tyre-test programme with Chris in the Cooper-Oldsmobile and the Whoosh-Bonk tyre-test car, so-named after Bruce McLaren conceived the idea of building a single-seater based around the corners and Oldsmobile engine and transmission from one of his CanAm sports cars. He sketched it all on the back of an envelope and went into the workshop to tell his team it would take no time at all to build it: 'Whoosh, bonk, and it's built!'

Harré could not understand why McLaren insisted on sticking with the aluminium-block Oldsmobile V8.

I'd ask him why he persevered with this bloody Olds engine. He'd tried to get it up to 5 litres with fuel injection, and spent a lot of time and money at Traco Engineering in Culver City, California, but the thing kept breaking and wouldn't run properly. Chris and I were scheduled for a three-day test at Silverstone with the M1B, the car styled by Michael Turner, the artist, so we went to a plumber's supply shop in Surbiton and bought some sheets of lead. We worked out how much heavier a Chev engine was than the Oldsmobile and how much heavier a ZF gearbox would be than the Hewland HD4. When we had finished the Firestone testing, we strapped the lead around the chassis frames each side of the engine to represent the increased engine weight and tied it all around the gearbox with lock-wire. Chris went out and drove more than 1 second a lap quicker with the Oldsmobile engine and all the extra lead weight. Bruce wouldn't believe it. He just *wouldn't* believe it. His pet theory was always that lightweight was the way to go. He had some ideas and they were fixed. He would go to the ends of the earth and he reckoned Amon had been driving at eleven-tenths to go quicker, because it *must* go slower if it was heavier. He thought Amon and I were bullshitting him but the Firestone timekeeper was an independent observer and Bruce eventually had to succumb to the Chev engine and the bigger gearbox .

Chris raced in a white helmet with a Kiwi on each side, one facing forwards, the other backwards, which prompted the observation that the design simply indicated the Amon talent for indecision. In 1965 an American helmet painter suggested a red, white and blue colour scheme, which subsequently became Chris's easily identifiable trademark.

In 1966 the Grand Prix formula doubled from 1.5 litres to 3 litres. Bruce McLaren was anxious to keep Chris in his team but he was defeated by his own bold decision to make his own 3-litre engine from a linered-down 4.2-litre 4-cam Indianapolis Ford V8. Bruce and Chris were both contracted Ford drivers and Bruce was anxious to involve Ford with his Formula One project. It seemed like a natural extension of their relationship, but unbeknown to Bruce there was already a Formula One Ford engine on the horizon. The problem, as far as Bruce was concerned, was that his engine was sourced from Ford of Britain, through Cosworth Engineering, and not from Dearborn in the USA. He had been aiming at the wrong arm of the Ford Motor Company.

The engine simply didn't work. It made the most glorious exhaust noise when it first appeared in Monaco but it had a pitiful amount of power and Bruce tried other engines while the team worked in desperation to make the Indy Ford competitive. Chris, meantime, put his racing career on hold. He was heading the Firestone test programme but was naturally anxious to race.

He drove a Cooper-Maserati in the French Grand Prix at Reims.

Cooper wanted to run three cars for some reason so I was driving a third car with John Surtees and Jochen Rindt. I was running down in the field, slipstreaming with Jochen, when my Cooper-Maserati started dramatically oversteering. Jochen kept coming out of the slipstream and pointing to the back of my car. Fuel was leaking out on to the left rear tyre. That was my only Grand Prix that season and I finished eighth, four laps behind after a series of pit stops.

Better was to come in CanAm racing, where Chris picked up placings in the works McLaren-Elva. He also earned from his involvement with the movie *Grand Prix*, which John Frankenheimer was shooting for MGM. 'They had a 2-litre Brabham-BRM in the fleet and I suggested to Frankenheimer that we enter it in the Grand Prix at Monza. I attempted to qualify, but didn't make it.'

Journalist Bill Gavin has explored the MGM Brabham-BRM saga:

Chris planned to buy the car, run it at Monza and then take it home for the Tasman Series. Half the money came from an MGM production man, but after Chris failed to qualify at Monza and the Tasman organisers failed to offer the right sort of starting money, Chris found out that his partner hadn't been able to afford the investment anyway. So Chris bought his ex-partner's share and took the full loss of the whole operation.

In typical Amon style, Chris initially signed with the 'wrong' movie company. There were two movies on the stocks, the other being made by Warner Brothers.

I actually signed with the Warner Brothers movie but then it was scrubbed so I ended up with MGM and *Grand Prix*. Because I didn't have a car in Formula One, I ended up doing more and more work on the film, driving the special stripped Ford GT40 that Frankenheimer had set up as a camera car with monitors inside the cockpit and mountings for cameras all over it. We had a sort of trailer hitch on the back, which meant I could tow some of the movie stars in a single-seater car hooked on the back with a camera aimed at them. They sat there twirling the wheel and looking as though they were doing it for real. When one or two of the stars were being less than cooperative on the set, Frankenheimer encouraged me to go a little harder, and if you got carried away a bit, the Ford would be sliding and you'd actually flick the towed car over the verge. It was wonderful watching the expression on their faces.

There was a bit of artistic licence in *Grand Prix* but they attempted to be fairly accurate and the stories behind the plots were reasonably true to life. The characters were named to sound like real drivers. James Garner was 'Pete Aaron', which was meant to sound like 'Amon', and he wore my helmet colours.

Some of the stars didn't want to know about racing, but James Garner was quite good, and very keen, too, and we became friends. Actually, we had an enormous amount of fun making the movie, quite a lot of which doesn't bear repeating.

Bruce and Chris effectively lost and won with Ford in 1966. The Formula One engine project was an expensive disaster but the two Kiwis paired up in the Ford team to win Le Mans, pipping the sister car of team-mates Denny Hulme and Ken Miles in what was supposed to be a dead heat.

The racing world looks back on those days and regards the Kiwis as a close-knit trio, but Chris says it wasn't quite like that.

I knew Bruce and Denny in the early days, but not very well. People forget that I was three or four years behind them. Bruce and I had talked on a couple of occasions but we had no real contact before I started driving for him. I certainly didn't know him very well. I probably hadn't met Denny at all by then. Denny didn't socialise a lot, and the same could be said for Bruce as well then, I suppose.

Plus the fact that Bruce and Denny were married and Chris was an enthusiastic, eligible, international bachelor sportsman.

The inaugural running of the CanAm sports-car series in Canada and the USA in 1966 gave Chris a further taste of horsepower, the thrill he had so enjoyed since his early days with the 250F Maserati in New Zealand. The first race was at Sainte Jovite, in Quebec, in September. The front row of the grid more or less told the story. John Surtees was on pole in the Lola T70, Bruce McLaren was in the middle of the front row in the McLaren M11B, and Chris was on the outside in the other works McLaren.

Chris stormed into the lead off the start but before the lap was out he was off the road and then into the pits with sticking throttles and a damaged nose spoiler. The situation seemed to light his fuse. Surtees was in command, with Bruce, trying as he might, unable to find a way past. Chris's stop cost him a lap-and-a-half, but as he came storming back he made up 48 seconds in 53 laps, coming right up on the tail of his team owner, who was still trying to overtake the former motorcycle champion in the Lola. Bruce waved Chris through.

Despite being fired up with the adrenaline of his charge through the field, Chris could not find a way past Surtees either, so he settled for a new lap record instead. In fact he was still a lap behind, so he was classified third behind Surtees and Bruce. The charge had been well worth the effort. His record was over a second inside Surtees' pole position lap time.

Next round was on the Bridgehampton circuit on Long Island, New

York. Texan Jim Hall had arrived with his winged Chaparral and he claimed pole from Surtees' Lola, with Bruce McLaren on the outside. Chris was on the second row beside Phil Hill's Chaparral. The Chaparral challenge fell apart, Dan Gurney winning in his Lola with Chris hard on his heels and Bruce third.

For the race at Mosport Park, back in Canada, Gurney maintained his series pace on pole with the Lola. Chris was second fastest and Bruce third, completing the front row. A quirk of the regulations took timing only from Thursday's practice, regardless of better laps on later days. Hall was relegated to 10th in the Chaparral, and Surtees to 11th. This was the catalyst for a huge accident on the first turn, and in a race restart Gurney led until Chris slipped past and there were three Kiwis out in front — Chris and Bruce in the McLarens and Denny Hulme in a Lola. They maintained this order for nearly half the race, by which time Phil Hill was running slowly with a problem in the Chaparral. 'He simply didn't see me and cut across in front of me, putting me up a bank,' recalls Chris. 'I was young enough then to still be disappointed about things like that. It was one of the races that I really thought I was going to win and I was gutted.'

The others had a variety of problems, and Mark Donohue scored his first CanAm win in a Lola. He would dominate the series in the early 1970s with the fearsome turbocharged Penske Porsche 917s.

The series switched to California with the race at Laguna Seca, a two-heat event won overall by Phil Hill for Chaparral from Bruce's McLaren. Riverside was next. Bruce was on pole from Surtees' Lola but Chris was down in the fourth row of the 2-2-2 grid. Both McLarens retired with engine failure.

The series finale was at Las Vegas, where the winged Chaparrals claimed the front row from Chris (for McLaren), Surtees and Stewart (for Lola) and Bruce (McLaren). The wings failed on both Chaparrals, Chris broke his transmission and Surtees won from Bruce. Final point standings showed Surtees and Donohue first and second respectively in Lolas, Bruce third in his McLaren, Phil Hill and Jim Hall fourth and fifth in the Chaparrals and Chris sixth for McLaren.

The CanAm series was obviously an important growth area in international racing, and the Chaparrals had proved, if proof were necessary, that winged sophistication and complication didn't necessarily spell success. The McLaren men reckoned that being fast enough and finishing would get the job done, and they dominated the series until the early 1970s.

Another one-off race for Chris that year was an Indy event on the Mount Fuji circuit in Japan with Jimmy Clark, Graham Hill, Jackie Stewart and several of the regular oval-track drivers. The flight to Japan left from Indianapolis, and Chris remembers that when it was delayed by six or seven hours the four Formula One drivers played a round of golf on the course at the Speedway while the American drivers spent the time in the bar.

Most of them were absolutely plastered by the time the flight left. We were no sooner off the ground than the fun began. The United States Auto Club officials were all up in first class and we were all down the back. Bobby Unser was setting off firecrackers in the cabin! We'd have been locked up if he'd done it these days. I can't imagine how we weren't then.

In his book *Grand Prix Greats*, Nigel Roebuck reproduced Chris's account of the event:

It was us against the USAC regulars, and the whole thing was done on a pretty tight budget — I mean, we were supposed to go up to the circuit by train and then bus! Happily though, Graham knew the Rolls-Royce agent in Tokyo and he laid on a Silver Wraith or something for us, complete with chauffeur. That was great, sweeping past the USAC brigade in their bus and giving them the royal wave! They didn't like us at all . . .

There was a hairpin at Fuji and I don't think most of the Americans had ever had to deal with one before. At least it didn't seem that way. Qualifying was in their style, one at a time, and the first six or seven just never made it round at all. Graham, Jackie and I sat in the pits, awaiting our turn and getting more and more hysterical. Every time we'd hear an Offenhauser screaming down to the hairpin absolutely flat, then a violent screeching of locked wheels, then a brief silence — then finally *BOOF!* As they clobbered the bank! A couple of minutes would then elapse before some red-faced American would walk in, scowling at us . . .

I had an old Vollstedt for that race, a car built by a very nice guy called Rolla Vollstedt. It was pretty much based on an early Indy Cooper and actually wasn't a bad car. It was set up with the usual off-set Indy-type suspension, which meant that it didn't like right-hand corners all that much, but apart from that it was pretty good apart from the pedals, which were arranged brake-throttle-clutch. From memory I qualified fourth or fifth, the fastest three being Jimmy, Jackie and Graham, who had cars with conventional suspension. I got going quite well in the race and I had a good old dice with Mario Andretti for third place, which ended with me up on top of a bank.

I was lapping a guy called Chuck Hulse, who was in one of those old front-engined Indy Roadsters, most of which didn't have mirrors. Not that mirrors would have made a lot of difference to this guy, actually — apparently he was blind in the right eye and also deaf in the right ear! Yes, you've got it — I went to overtake him on the right . . . For reasons I never quite understood, he suddenly elected to turn sharp right and that was the end of my race. He had absolutely no depth of vision whatever — apparently, they said, because he'd been badly injured in a sprint-car accident years before.

5

A dead heat to Ford by 20 metres: high jinks at Le Mans

The Le Mans 24-hour race in 1966 was the high point in Chris Amon's motor-racing career. It was an enjoyable victory for him and Bruce McLaren in the Ford GT, but it was a hugely controversial result for the Ford Motor Company, with Henry Ford II and his entourage watching over events on the French circuit. In fact, from a corporate point of view it was of little importance who won the race — providing they were driving a Ford — but it was of huge importance in the pit lane to a variety of people for a variety of reasons. Texan racing entrepreneur Carroll Shelby and his team management had an agenda that did not match that of Bruce and his junior Kiwi co-driver.

The differences began with commercial tyre contracts. While the rest of the Ford team was contracted to Goodyear, Bruce was doing European race development work for rival American company Firestone, endlessly successful at Indianapolis but very much testing the water in Formula One and sports-car racing with the fledgling McLaren operation. It was a measure of Bruce's importance to the Ford Le Mans project that he was entered in a Goodyear-sponsored car fitted with Firestone tyres. But there was a proviso that if the car won, Firestone could not advertise the fact. As it turned out, the Firestone tyres failed and Goodyear made a feast of their success advertising with the Firestone drivers.

The Amon adventures at Le Mans have been well documented. As we have seen, the race organisers refused Chris's entry in 1963 on the grounds that he was too young, despite the fact that he had just raced in the

Belgian Grand Prix at Spa and completed Le Mans practice in a works Sunbeam Alpine entered by the Rootes Group.

After that I had a sort of love-hate relationship with the race. It was an event that I never really looked forward to because it was very hard work and there were only two drivers per car in those days. But once you got to Le Mans and became part of the whole atmosphere you got swept up in the spirit of the event with hundreds of thousands of spectators and, yeah, I guess I somehow enjoyed it despite my misgivings before the race each year.

My first drive for Shelby was at Le Mans in 1964, when I drove a Daytona Cobra coupé with Jochen Neerpasch, but the alternator failed and the battery went flat. In 1965 Phil Hill and I drove a GT40 and Bruce and Ken Miles shared the other Shelby entry. The gearboxes failed on both. They did tell us that the gearboxes were weak, and as we were waiting to run across the track at the start, Bruce said, 'Just take it easy — don't take off with too much vigour.' You should have seen a photo of the start — McLaren had more black rubber behind his Ford than me, but we both left plenty. I led on to the Mulsanne Straight, and Bruce slipstreamed me and came past, and I can remember coming out of the White House corner before the pits and looking in the mirror. The nearest Ferrari was 500 yards behind and we were *gone*. They were the competition. Our gearbox packed up about two in the morning and I think Bruce's went before that.

Chris remembers driving back to England in a red Mustang convertible after the 1965 Le Mans race with me as a passenger. I have no recollection of the trip, but he says he remembers it vividly.

We had left the circuit and we were cruising through the French back-country roads and you were getting very agitated. I asked you what the matter was and you said, 'Why in the hell don't you slow down a bit? We're doing over 120 mph,' and I said, 'A hundred and twenty? We're only idling.' After driving at high speed for so long in the race, I thought we were just having a quiet drive through the country.

At the beginning of 1966 we went to Daytona, where Shelby had three Fords and Holman and Moody also had three. After our gearbox problems the year before we didn't know whether they'd last or not, so we decided to take it easy. Talk about egg on our faces. We were fifth because we pussyfooted. After four hours the other guys had lapped us three times, but we thought that at the end of the 24 hours we'd still be there and they wouldn't, but of course they all kept going. When we got to Le Mans, Bruce said, 'We're not screwing around like that again, we're going to *go* for it!'

Funnily enough I only ever made it through the night twice. In 1969 my Ferrari wouldn't start so I got away almost last, way, way back, and I caught up with John Woolf in one of the first of those big 917 Porsche customer cars. The thing looked as squirly as hell and I almost got past him at the end of the Mulsanne Straight, but we only had 3 litres and the Porsche was a 4.5-litre. I was quite concerned following him and then he lost the whole lot in White House, which was a bloody quick 150 mph corner, and hit the bank. I'd backed off. The Porsche just blew apart — a ball of flame and pieces everywhere. The fuel tank came across the road and straight under my car and everything was on fire. I had a tank full of burning fuel under my car and I was still doing 170 mph. It took a long time to lose speed and I couldn't see what the hell I was doing. I had my belts undone, but as soon as I got the door open on the closed coupé the flames came straight in. I waited what seemed like an eternity for the Ferrari to slow down but it was still going quite quickly when I launched myself out. I didn't realise it at the time but Frank Gardner had made a bad start as well and he bloody nearly ran me over on the track. He said that at the last minute he saw someone launch out of the ball of flame in front of him. The car careered to the side of the road and burned itself out and I walked back to the pits. I was quite OK but it was a horrific shunt.

Le Mans started at 4 o'clock on Saturday afternoon, and the worst thing that could happen to you was that you got through to about 8 o'clock or 9 o'clock the next morning and then something broke on the car. It happened to me in 1971, when I was driving a Matra with Jean-Pierre Beltoise. The car gave up at about 10 o'clock on the Sunday morning. We'd been up all night sharing the driving and then it stopped, and when we were teamed again in a Matra in 1972, I said to Jean-Pierre, 'If we're not going to finish the race this year, let's make sure we stop early.' The engine threw a rod on the first lap and I was back in London in time for dinner.

At Le Mans in 1966 Bruce and I decided we weren't going to worry about pacing ourselves. We were just going to get on with it and *race*. We were running Firestones while the rest of the team were on Goodyears, and we had major tyre problems in the first hour-and-a-half and lost a lot of time. We started on intermediate tyres because it was sort of showery and the bloody things started chunking. Bruce had done the start and after 10 laps or so he came in with great chunks of tread off the tyres. This happened every few laps, and I remember sitting there thinking we had *no* chance. Shelby said, 'It's up to you guys. You're contracted to Firestone but we've got plenty of Goodyears sitting here.' So we switched. It was unfortunate for Firestone.

Because we had got ourselves well behind, we said to hell with it, we're gonna go for it for the rest of the race. And we drove as though it was a Grand Prix distance and we had a lot of fun.

You don't hear a lot about *fun* in motor racing these days, so it's interesting to reflect on a pair of New Zealand drivers who could enjoy themselves in the chase for a famous win in one of the world's most famous races.

With about two hours to go there was nobody able to tough it out with the three Fords in front, and the decision was made to hold station because we were beyond challenge. It was pouring with rain and there was a genuine desire among the Ford hierarchy not to take any chances. Then somebody had the bright idea that it might be nice to have a dead heat, but I think the organisers got wind of that and decided it wasn't going to be a dead heat. It didn't really detract from anything as far as I was concerned because we'd been way behind, we'd caught up, and Bruce was driving the last stint. I had a feeling that Bruce had made up his mind that we were going to win anyway, despite any arrangements the team was trying to make about crossing the line in a photo finish.

It is well worth considering the importance to Ford of the 1966 Le Mans victory, regardless of the variance in accounts of the chaos of the disputed finish, which featured three New Zealanders in the first two Fords. Denny Hulme shared second place with British ex-pat Ken Miles, who was based in California and had headed Shelby's development programme with the G40s. Miles was devastated, in tears at the finish, claiming that he had been cheated of his rightful win. Hulme was more philosophical, saying he would have done what Bruce had done given the chance of a win.

The Le Mans win was Henry Ford's way of sticking two fingers up to Enzo Ferrari, who had spurned Ford's attempt in the early 1960s to buy his Italian company and turn it into a performance branch of the Ford Motor Company. Ford had countered by buying another GT racing concept, from British designer Eric Broadley, who had created a stylish mid-engined Lola GT and was commissioned to progress the design into what would be the first Ford GT40 in 1964 — a monocoque centre section with a 4-cam 4.2-litre Indianapolis Ford V8 in the back, so titled because it was just 40 inches from the road to the top of the roof.

By 1966, working with Ford, Shelby had masterminded the Cobra project. The Cobra was the first blue-oval GT to towel the Ferraris in long-distance GT endurance events. Shelby had honed a Mark II version of the GT40, installing a 7-litre Ford V8 and ensuring a measure of reliability that would give Ford four further years of domination in endurance racing. Ford won both the Daytona 24-hour race and the Sebring 12-hour race 1-2-3, and although they did the same again at Le Mans, it was the finishing order of the first two cars that caused a historic controversy — and Bruce and Chris were major actors in the drama, which would have been deemed too implausible for a movie script.

'Ford didn't cost Ken the race at Le Mans, I did — and I regret it to this day,' confesses Shelby, who himself won at Le Mans driving for Aston Martin in 1959. He grew up through American and European racing in the 1950s and created the legendary Cobra from an almost vintage British AC sports car on the verge of sales extinction, giving it the ultimate revitalisation with the installation of the big American engine.

They [Ford] came to me and said, 'Who do you think should win the race?' I thought, 'Well, hell, Ken's been leading for all these hours, he should win the race.'

I looked at [Ford competition director and GT40 project chief]

Leo Beebe and said, 'What do you think ought to happen, Leo?' He said, 'I don't know. I'd kind of like to see all three of them cross the line together.'

Leo didn't tell me what to say or what to do, so I said, 'Oh, hell, let's do it that way then,' not knowing that the French would interpret the rules the way they did.

Ken [and Denis] should have won the race, and in most everyone's mind he did win the race. I take full responsibility for it, and I'm very sorry for it because Ken was killed at Riverside [testing for Ford] two months later. Every time you go racing, you put your reputation on the line.

Yet another version of events is supplied by author Karl Ludvigsen, who was working in the upper echelons of the Ford Motor Company in the 1960s. In his book *Bruce McLaren — Life and Legacy of Excellence*, he wrote:

The McLaren/Amon Ford was comfortably leading the other team car under an 'EZE' pit signal and running 30 seconds slower than they were able, to protect their positions. But when Bruce pitted with three hours to go, he found the rival Ford hot on his heels: 'In the previous five laps, Miles had caught up about 30 seconds, when we were supposed to be lapping at four minutes and no faster or slower. He also made a pit stop and handed over to Denny.' Watching his own pit stop as Chris took over, Bruce was amazed to see a Goodyear man shout for a wheel to be changed. 'At the time I thought there was something fishy about it, but I didn't realise until I thought about it that he hadn't looked at the wheel.

'Fifteen minutes ago we had been 30 seconds ahead, but after the burst of speed by Miles and the suspicious tyre change we were now about 40 seconds behind and supposed to lap calmly at the same speed until the 4pm finish.'

Carroll Shelby told Bruce that team orders were for the car leading after the last pit stop to be the winner. Bruce took the matter to the Ford men, who called the top shots and suggested that a photo finish would earn Ford more publicity. They agreed. Bruce reckoned that Henry Ford wasn't really too concerned who won as long as one of his cars did, and Bruce didn't see why Chris and he, as Firestone-contracted drivers in Shelby's Goodyear-sponsored team, should be penalised. He later wrote to his father, Les, in Auckland: 'I didn't think ten minutes of politics would win a 24-hour race, but there you are. Nice guys don't win ball games, they say.'

In his 1968 book *The Racing Fords*, author Hans Tanner offers yet another view of the famous finish:

By a prearranged plan the Fords of McLaren and Miles arrived with headlights ablaze, in as near a dead heat as they could judge, with the other Ford of Bucknum just behind. It was an impressive and undisputed victory. The celebration was somewhat damped, however, when the timekeepers announced that McLaren and Amon had won, a dead heat being impossible as the cars had started at 4pm on Saturday with the Miles/Hulme car already some yards ahead of the starting grid so that as they arrived side by side on the same lap on Sunday at 4pm, the McLaren/Amon car must have covered a greater distance in the 24 hours, the difference being quoted as 20 metres. The staging by the Shelby team had backfired.

Chris Amon has the final say:

Bruce made bloody sure he was in front. He made absolutely sure that it was no dead heat because he crossed the line two or three lengths ahead of Miles. Ken was quite upset about it.

It rained on and off for the whole race and I find it difficult to sit back now and think that we actually averaged 125 mph for 24 hours when 15 hours of the 24 would have been in the wet. They were *so* fast, those 7-litre Mk IIs. We were doing 220-something miles an hour down the Mulsanne Straight.

The winning Kiwis were the focus of adulation.

After we had been up on the platform with Henry Ford, we went to the Ford camp for some more champagne — then to Goodyear for more champagne — then to Shell for more champagne — then to Moet et Chandon for some of their champagne — and then to Martini for still more champagne. It took us about three hours to get back to the hotel, and one of the most wonderful things was to get into a hot bath.

Looking back over his long career in the upper tiers of international motor racing, does Chris think the 1966 Le Mans win was his most important?

I suppose on paper, prestige-wise, it was, but in terms of satisfaction I never really got as much out of long-distance races as I did from Formula One. Most of the race you were having to try and be strategic in that you couldn't beat the hell out of the thing the whole time. You weren't at full pace, you were trying to conserve the car. There *was* a satisfaction from doing it, and a lot of the successful long-distance drivers had a strategy whereby they could pace themselves, pace the car and do a good job in winning and get a lot of satisfaction out of that. But I'm afraid I liked to get out there and go for it. Apart from anything else, when I was pacing myself I used to find it hard to keep my concentration, but there were other drivers who specialised in that sort of thing. When I went to Le Mans with Ferrari in 1967, Mike Parkes was absolutely brilliant. He used to work out the lap times that he needed to be doing and stick to them, and quite often he was successful.

6 Meet Mr Ferrari: the lure of a legend

I was at Watkins Glen, spectating at the US Grand Prix, when Keith Ballisat from Shell approached me in the lobby of the Glen Motor Inn. He asked me what I was doing the following weekend and I said I had a CanAm race, so he said, 'What about Sunday night, Monday and Tuesday?' I said, 'Probably not a lot,' and he said, 'Would you like to come over to Italy with me and meet Mr Ferrari?' Talk about a bolt from the blue. It took me about two whole seconds to say 'Yes!' Actually I was in a difficult situation, because Bruce wanted me to stay at McLaren, but driving for Ferrari was also a boyhood ambition of mine — I'd sort of loved Ferraris from the time I'd got interested in racing.

Enzo Ferrari entertained the new young driver but refused to say more than 'maybe' about a Formula One drive.

It was the usual old story of four drivers for two cars in Formula One. There was no problem with an endurance sports-car drive, and he suggested there would be no problem about Formula One either, but he couldn't or wouldn't put it in writing. I never did find out why, but after a couple of endurance races he was as good as his word and I was entered for the first Grand Prix of the season, at Monaco.

I was absolutely in awe of the Old Man, as I think most people were. He was actually quite good at putting me at ease. We did the contractual negotiations then went over to the Cavallino restaurant, across the road from the factory at Maranello. We had a wonderful lunch and I sat there being very good, drinking mineral water with all this good food and wine on the table, and he said through his interpreter that it was always interesting having the first lunch with a new driver. He said that in the 1950s Mike Hawthorn had had lunch and drunk a bottle of his best malt whisky, having signed the contract half an hour before. He always took a keen interest in his drivers' relations with the opposite sex. He had a superb intelligence set-up; in fact, I think he knew more about what we were doing than we did.

It was Chris's first taste of Formula One in the grand way of doing things. There had been the promise of Formula One at McLaren but it had been little more than a possibility in the short term, given the succession of disasters with the engines in 1966 and into 1967.

'The sheer scale of Ferrari in those days was amazing compared with anything I'd seen. McLaren probably had 15–20 on the staff, and so did Lotus and the other British teams, but in my first year at Ferrari there were 100 on the staff in the racing department. That was mind-boggling. Virtually every part of the car was built in the factory.'

Enzo always did the best deal on the day, and when Jacky Ickx signed for the 1968 season, Chris soon found that the young Belgian was getting far more money than he was.

Ickx chose not to live in Italy, let alone Modena, and as a result I did all the testing and setting up of both cars in Formula One and Formula Two. I never had any problems with him but when I found out he was on a retainer of $30,000, I was livid. I stewed on it for days, trying to figure out how I was going to confront the Old Man.

He was always very approachable and available, sometimes too available, so one day I got up a head of steam and went and asked why Ickx was on a retainer of 30 grand when I was only getting a share of the purse. He looked at me and said, 'But you never asked.' So I did right then, and he agreed on the spot. It was the quickest 30 grand I ever made.

The Italian press always baited foreign drivers at Ferrari.

I had a sort of love-hate relationship with them which was probably more hate than love, I think. It was difficult for them because Ferrari was going through a fairly average period during most of my time there. If we won — not that I ever did in a single-seater — it was the car, and if we lost, it was down to the driver. And it wasn't just the journalists. There were certain people within the team who had great difficulty in being convinced that the car wasn't up to scratch.

If you're driving for Ferrari and living in Italy, you can live like royalty. The whole of Italy was behind motor racing, and I had three wonderful years there — three of the best years of my life, to be honest.

Back at McLaren, Chris thought Bruce felt betrayed.

He felt that his Formula One team was on the brink of getting it right, and I guess he also felt he'd invested a couple of years in me too. We always got on well, but I don't think it was ever quite as close as it used to be.

I went to Daytona for testing with Ferrari in December 1966 with the three other contracted drivers — Lorenzo Bandini, Michael Parkes and Ludovico Scarfiotti. It was like stepping into a hornets' nest, with all of us knowing there were only two seats for Formula One, maybe three at some races. We did three days of testing and it became apparent that Lorenzo and I were fastest. We did a hell of a lot of laps, and it was important for me psychologically to prove myself for one of those Formula One seats.

Ferrari didn't send any cars to South Africa for the season-opener, their world-championship bid starting instead at Monaco. Lorenzo and Chris were the chosen drivers. By the time the race was run in early May, the Bandini–Amon combination had already won two of the three major sports-car races in the 4-litre P4 Ferrari. In the 24-hour race at Daytona, in February, the Ferraris shattered any hope Ford might have had of winning on its home ground, the Italian–Kiwi duo finishing three laps clear of Scarfiotti and Parkes in the other works car. No Fords were entered in the 1000-kilometre race at Monza in April, and while the high-winged Chaparral 2F provided opposition, the works P4s again dominated, with Lorenzo and Chris once more leading Scarfiotti and Parkes home in the five-hour event.

It was typical of Chris's turbulent fortune that he didn't get to drive in his official debut with the Ferrari team in the nonchampionship Race of Champions at Brands Hatch before the season proper began.

I was driving down to Brands Hatch in my Sunbeam Tiger on the day before practice to check in and see the team. David Hall was with me when this woman turned right across in front of me and we hit amidships. David smashed his head on the screen and was badly cut. I had braced myself against the steering wheel and bent it in half. We ended up at the same hospital as the woman who had hit us and it turned out that she had thousands of pounds strapped to her body. She was booked to go abroad that night and was obviously smuggling currency, so she'd had her mind on things other than driving her car. I had injured my arm and ankle and bruised my ribs, and the next day I drove a couple of laps and realised that I'd have to pull out. So much for my first drive with Ferrari.

That week *Autosport* wrote:

Amon's ability to scratch round the tight little 2.65-mile circuit is undisputed and he would have got the V12 Ferrari round very quickly. As it was, he had to drive with one hand and could not use his right foot on the brakes very effectively, so doing his best in the two practice periods he decided it would be unwise to try and race in his battered condition and withdrew, leaving Bandini and Scarfiotti to uphold the honour of Maranello.

Chris made his Ferrari Grand Prix debut at Monaco, the team's season-opener in 1967, and witnessed the fiery crash that resulted in the death of Lorenzo Bandini. 'I'd got to know him pretty well, and he was very supportive of me in the team, which was very important politically. His death probably spurred me on because it was fairly obvious that I was quicker than the other two [Scarfiotti and Parkes] and so it really put more responsibility on me, which was probably good in the long run.'

Lorenzo crashed at the quayside chicane late in the race in pursuit of Denny Hulme's Brabham, his Ferrari hitting hay bales, overturning and catching fire. He died later from burns.

I think it was sheer fatigue. It was a long race, the thick end of three hours, and it was very hot that day. I know by about the 75th lap I was actually starting to get cold in the car, which meant that I was totally dehydrated. I'm sure he went through the same thing and it

∧
Spinning off near the end of the 1968 Teretonga International (above) just before Frank Gardner spun off at the same spot (below).

∧
Drifting the Ferrari at Oulton Park.

NICK LOUDEN

∧
In the 1.6-litre V6 Ferrari F2 at Zolder, 1968.

∧
Starting from pole at Zandvoort in 1968. Jochen Rindt and Graham Hill complete
the front row.

GRAND PRIX PHOTO

∧
The 1968 winged Ferrari in the Monza pits with Mauro Forghieri in attendence.

ATTUALFOTO

^
Chris Amon at the 1969 New Zealand Grand Prix at Pukekohe.

PEACH WEMYSS

^
Chris qualified second for the 1969 Monaco Grand Prix and ran well until the differential
broke. The Ferrari was never again a competitive package in 1969.

^
Chris took the podium six times for Ferrari, the last in the 1969 Dutch Grand Prix.

^
All over. The last time Chris Amon raced a Formula One Ferrari was at Silverstone in the 1969 British Grand Prix.

∧
The line-up for the Grand Prix drivers' cricket match of 1969 included Dickie Attwood, Piers Courage, Jochen Rindt, Graham Hill, Pedro Rodrigues, Denny Hulme, Charles Lucas, Robin Widdows, Peter Procter, Innes Ireland, Bruce McLaren, Chris Amon, Stirling Moss and Colin Chapman.

TED WALKER

∧
Graham Hill, Chris Amon and Derek Bell.

ATTUALFOTO

∧
Chris Amon, nearing the end of his tether with Ferrari.

AUTOCAR

∧
Bruce McLaren and Chris Amon with their Indy 500 car; McLaren had used the wing with great success in sports car races and hoped for a similar result at Indy.

was purely a lapse of concentration that caused him to run wide and hit the bales.

Lorenzo's death hit Chris hard because they had become good friends. In Nigel Roebuck's splendid book *Chasing the Title*, Chris recalls:

I was never a great one for believing in premonitions, but the Wednesday before the race at Monaco made me wonder. We went off for lunch in the mountains, and on the drive back Lorenzo seemed very reflective, very aware of the simple things in life — you know, flowers, the fact that it was spring, and so on. On the way down, he saw an old man fishing by the side of the road, and he stopped, just to watch him quietly for a while. It's difficult to convey what I'm getting at, but it was almost as if he were savouring life, as if he knew something was going to happen. I'll never forget that day.

Lorenzo's death was all the more difficult to accept because he and Chris had formed such a bond within the team. 'I had the initial impression that he might be difficult, because of the incident in the 1964 Mexican Grand Prix when the English press concluded that he had rammed Graham Hill's BRM on purpose. But he wasn't the controversial character I expected. He was absolutely charming.'

Chris spoke almost no Italian and Lorenzo spoke only limited English but the two got on well. They drove together from Modena to Monaco for the fateful race.

I remember sitting in his car for a couple of hours while he said his goodbyes to his mistress. In the end we didn't arrive in Monaco until after 2.00 a.m., with the first practice due to start in only a few hours. I didn't get to bed until around 3.00 a.m. and I remember thinking that this was hardly the ideal start to my Ferrari Formula One career.

Chris and Lorenzo were due to fly to Indianapolis for qualifying immediately after the race at Monaco.

Because of the terrible accident I had to make the trip alone. I knew before I left Monte Carlo that his chances of survival were minimal, so it was a miserable journey. Then, on the Wednesday morning, I turned up at the track to try my car, only to be told that Lorenzo had died of his burns. That upset me a lot, even though I suppose I had been expecting it.

I went out in the car, which wasn't especially competitive, and a rear upright broke. I was running fairly quickly when this happened and the car went into a series of spins, which seemed to last forever. After 900 feet of this, the car finally clouted the wall, and I got out without a scratch, but the thing was, it lasted so long that I had time to think, time to get frightened. After the news of Bandini's death, all sorts of things were flashing through my mind while I just sat there, waiting for it to hit. The car was wrecked, so I didn't drive it in the race, which didn't bother me overly, I must admit.

Come Le Mans, Chris had a new co-driver. 'I was sharing an open P4 at Le Mans with Nino Vacarella. I elected to use the open car because it was more comfortable — and it was fortunate I did, because it was easier to get out of.'

The Ferrari team was anxious to take the game to Ford at Le Mans: they were going to win for Lorenzo. That was Chris's ambition as he went back to Le Mans — and the fact that he had won the classic race for Ford the previous year and was now leading the Italian opposition made him all the more determined.

We were hanging in there in second or third and the other Ferrari of Parkes and Scarfiotti was in there somewhere as well. We were about seven hours into the race, just before midnight, and I'd come past the pits and was going into Dunlop Corner when I felt a bit of a twitch at the rear. It was a puncture and by the time I got on to the Mulsanne Straight the tyre was really flat and I could hear all sorts of graunching noises, which meant that the suspension upright and the rim were starting to grind on the road, so I had no choice but to stop and change the wheel.

He pulled off to one side of the long straight and opened the engine cover to get at the spare, a get-you-home space-saver that only just scraped inside the letter of the regulations. He laughs as he describes the on-car tool-kit.

There was a sort of jack, a torch and a wheel hammer to knock the centre-lock spinner off. The first thing I discovered was that the batteries in the torch were flat, but there were plenty of cars coming past with their headlights blazing so I had light on and off — occasional illumination at 200 mph.

I got the jack out and started to crank it up. It actually worked after a fashion, and the next step was to get the wheel hammer, wait for a blaze of headlights and take a shot at the centre-lock wheel-nut. I swung at it and the head flew off the hammer, disappearing into the night and the track-side ditch. So I'm crawling around in the ditch looking for the head off this bloody hammer at one in the morning . . .

He shakes with laughter again at the recollection of the comic-opera situation, seemingly so typical of his time with Ferrari.

I was obviously going to have to drive it back to the pits somehow, so I packed the kit away, got back in, fired up and drove away relatively slowly down the straight — but I was probably still doing 100 mph and the tyre was disintegrating, flapping wildly. There were sparks showering back from the suspension upright, and I assume what eventually happened was that a fuel line was knocked off one of the pannier-type fuel tanks just in front of the rear wheels. The whole car just went up in flames — *BOOF!*

I had been tooling down the right-hand side of the track anyway, and I aimed it for the ditch. It was getting bloody warm by that stage, so I jumped out, thinking I had almost stopped, but I was probably still doing 50 mph and I ended up somersaulting down the ditch while the Ferrari rolled another 100 metres along the road before it came to a stop not far from a marshals' post.

The marshals could see the flames from the car, which was now well alight, and they came running. There were four marshals and three Gendarmes, and they soon had the fire out and were searching frantically for the driver — me. They were looking around in the ditch, wondering where I was, and I remember walking up the ditch, feeling a bit battered, and tapping a Gendarme on the shoulder and saying, 'Here I am.' Poor guy. He bloody near died of fright.

Chris immersed himself in the Italian lifestyle. While there was no contractual requirement for him to visit the factory on a daily basis, or even live in Italy for that matter, it was something he believed it was important to do. He would wander down to his local barber every morning for a shave and to get the local gossip. It gave him a buzz that his barber used to shave the famous Tazio Nuvolari. Perhaps Enzo Ferrari also appreciated his new young driver's sense of history.

Some nights he would phone me at my apartment and insist we have dinner. He would always announce himself as 'Engineer'. We would often go up into the mountains above Maranello for lunch. It was a little cooler up there and the restaurant always made a big fuss of him. The Old Man had a 2 + 2 Berlinetta that he loved to drive and rev to well beyond the red line. He was close to 70, but he could still push it along a bit. Pepino, his old riding mechanic from his racing days in the 1920s, was still with him. His job was to clean the car every day and warm it up before heading off for lunch. The Old Man also had this poodle called Dick that would ride in the back with Pepino while he drove and I rode alongside.

He would never eat with Pepino. He and I would sit at one table while Pepino sat with Dick. I've been a dog lover and owner all my life, but Dick was the only dog I'd ever seen eat fruit salad — and tomatoes. The Old Man would drink the best part of a bottle of wine while I drank mineral water. Then he'd have a couple of malt whiskies. The drive home was always extremely erratic, and I have clear memories of Pepino and Dick being thrown about, sliding from side to side across the back seat. There was always a lot of horn-blowing, donkeys being scattered, people being scattered, and I used to think that if my time had come, at least I was going in good company.

While he was at Ferrari Chris initially had a Fiat 125 as his personal road car. This was followed by a second-hand Alfa Romeo Giulia Super, and then a silver Ferrari 330GT. 'It was a 2 + 2 V12 and it only cost me about $4000. I kept it in England but it was a bloody useless thing. The plugs would foul up constantly and in London traffic you'd soon be running a V11 and eventually a V10. Or less.'

He was more enthusiastic about Mini Coopers. He bought his first from Cooper Formula One driver Tony Maggs, but his favourite was the special version he bought while with Ferrari.

The Mini designer, Alec Issigonis, was a great mate of Enzo's and he had three 1275s built with torque-converter automatic transmission. One was for Enzo, one for Stirling Moss and one for Lofty England at Jaguar. I managed to persuade them to build a fourth one for me and it was magic in central-London traffic.

In 1969 I bought a new 6.9-litre Mercedes-Benz 300 SEL. It was great until I headed off for a race and left it at an airport. When I returned and tried to start it, there was no antifreeze in it and it stopped with a clunk and the block split.

I claimed that Mercedes should have provided it with antifreeze as standard but they told me it was my problem. They fixed it eventually at their cost, but I decided that I never needed to own a Mercedes again after that.

The 1967 season was not the time to start out in Formula One with a Ferrari. It was another Brabham year, and Denny Hulme won the world championship before switching to McLaren for 1968 and luxuriating in the Formula One and CanAm rides that Chris would have enjoyed but for the lure of the Ferrari legend. Chris had started the season with the sniff of a promise of a Formula One drive, but soon found himself team leader, for what it was worth. He was the eternal third — in Monaco, at Spa, at Silverstone and on the Nürburgring. He had been in second place at Monaco but picked up a puncture with ten laps left and the stop cost him a place. At Spa he was running in company with Mike Parkes when the tall Englishman lost control and spun.

Chris told Nigel Roebuck:

> The BRMs always dropped oil at the beginning of a race. I was right behind Mike and had a bad moment on it too. He spun, and I backed off — which was a mistake, actually, because you're better keeping your foot on it. He spun backwards across the road and hit the bank, and then, instead of coming back onto the road, his car rolled along the bank. It was like a toy somersaulting over and over — just the most horrific bloody shunt you could imagine. Later they hung out a board telling me he was OK, but I didn't see it and drove the whole race assuming he was dead. Coming so soon after Bandini's accident, that had a profound effect on me. It totally destroyed poor old Scarfiotti. He never raced a Formula One Ferrari after that day.

In the French Grand Prix on the unloved short Le Mans 'Bugatti' circuit, Chris dropped out of third place with a broken throttle linkage. He was the sole Ferrari entry, and had the team to himself most of the summer.

The British Grand Prix at Silverstone saw him trapped behind Jack Brabham. It was a race that Ferrari regarded as an example of his driver's lack of 'tiger', being unwilling to accept that the car was short of power.

> In fact it was one of the most enjoyable races I ever had, but it was frustrating too. Every lap I'd come out of Jack's slipstream before Stowe and then have to drop back in again, because the Ferrari didn't have the steam to get by. Old Jack was playing with his mirrors early in the race — in fact, one fell off and whistled past my head. He lost the other one, too, and I've never quite known

whether he was adjusting them or trying to tear them off. He said he had a wheel out of balance and the mirrors were shaking. It was a very wide car, that Brabham, and Jack was throwing everything in the book at me: stones, grass, dirt — and mirrors, of course. I finally got by him when he ran a bit wide coming out of Woodcote with three laps to go. After that I started to catch Denny [Hulme] quickly but we ran out of laps and I was third behind Jimmy [Clark] and Denny.

At the Nürburgring Chris had a new, slightly lighter car, but it was still heavier than the frontrunners and short on power by 30 bhp. It was apparent that Chris was making up for these deficiencies with his talent. He closed on Brabham in the closing laps of the 14.8-mile circuit, fighting for second place, but there was no way past and he finished third half a second adrift while Hulme won one of his best races.

The Canadian Grand Prix was the first wet event of the season, and Chris was in immediate trouble, spinning on the warm-up lap and again early in the race. It teemed throughout, and the occasion isn't one Chris cares to recall, but he remembers Enzo Ferrari's comment when he got back to Maranello.

He never praised anyone if they had a good race but at the same time there was never any criticism from him if you had a bad race. I think the nearest he came to criticising a result of mine was after the Canadian Grand Prix when it poured with rain. The Firestone tyres were hopeless in the wet. I had lunch with the Old Man when I got back and he said to me, 'I feel like the Duke of Modena.' I didn't have a bloody clue who the Duke of Modena was and I asked someone afterwards what the Old Man was talking about. It turned out that the Duke of Modena had a mercenary army that only fought battles on fine days. The duke wouldn't fight in the rain. That was Ferrari's form of censure.

Monza usually brought out a Ferrari show of force, but this time Chris was the lone works entry and he soldiered through the race, battling a failing damper and enduring several spins before stopping for repairs and finishing a disconsolate seventh. Back in North America for the Grand Prix at Watkins Glen, he was up in second and challenging Jim Clark for the lead but lost oil pressure in the closing laps. Finally there was Mexico, where he was joined by Jonathan Williams. Chris qualified second to Clark's Lotus and was running second until he unaccountably ran short of fuel two laps from the flag and was relegated to a lowly ninth. Clark won the race and Denny Hulme the world championship.

During the season Chris had known that Jackie Stewart was becoming disillusioned with BRM and was pressing to get him into the Ferrari team. This came closer to happening than most people knew at the time. Stewart and Ferrari actually shook hands on a deal for 1968 but it fell apart before it reached contract stage. Ferrari had apparently reconsidered, thinking Stewart had asked for too great a retainer: 'Stewart asks for Maranello!' he told his team manager, Franco Lini, who was despatched to sign Jacky Ickx instead.

'I think Chris and I would have combined well if I had driven for Ferrari in 1968,' Jackie told me in the summer of 2002. 'You could never have said that Chris was underrated, it's just that somehow or other he always failed to close the loop. It's not a totally unusual thing with racing drivers.'

Chris told Alan Henry for his book *Ferrari — The Grand Prix Cars*: 'I suppose I was a bit on the lazy side and Jackie could have taken some of the testing off my shoulders. I also figured that if Jackie told them their V12s were short on power they might have believed him. I would have liked to have had Jackie in the team because it would have given me something to measure myself against.'

It would be two more years before Amon and Stewart raced identical cars — at March, in 1970.

7 Amon black magic: 'I never even won a race'

There were times during 1967 when the Ferrari flattered heroically to deceive, so the 1968 season could only be an improvement. It was worse. There were flashes of sheer brilliance, which are talked about whenever Chris Amon's ability is analysed, but they seemed to be one-offs, indications that driver and car could do it but that it was always the car that let down the driver.

The eight-race Tasman Series in New Zealand and Australia appealed to Chris, who was eager to perform in front of home crowds, and he arranged to have a special Ferrari based on the works Formula Two car but fitted with a 2.4-litre 285 bhp V6 Dino engine and entered under his own name. It was to be a summer-long battle with Jim Clark's 2.5-litre 330 bhp Lotus-Ford 49T. The two drivers ran wheel to wheel, trading wins. Chris won the New Zealand Grand Prix after Clark's engine failed, and won again the following weekend at Levin when Clark clipped a course marker trying to catch him and retired with damaged suspension.

'It was very nice to win at home, but at the time it was very nice to win *anywhere*, because we weren't having the greatest run in Formula One. But whilst winning my home Grand Prix was great, I really wanted to win a world-championship Grand Prix.'

Bruce Wilson, who had looked after Chris's first racing cars, joined the Tasman Ferrari team of Chris, Roger Bailey, Bill Bryce and the young Ferrari engineer Gianni Marelli, who had been responsible for the development of the Tasman car at the factory and to begin with was jealous of letting Wilson work on it. As Wilson recalls:

Once we established the fact that I was allowed even to check the water on this very special Ferrari and that you didn't really have to be a Ferrari employee to do it, we got on very well. I didn't blame him for being careful. It was an eye-opener for me to work on a car that was so well prepared and sorted out. I think it surprised everybody that Chris ran so well in practice against Jim Clark and the other internationals — and then to win the Grand Prix on his own merits was quite something.

We won again at Levin but we didn't fare too well against the power of Jimmy's Lotus on the wide-open spaces and long straights at Wigram. Gianni was on the phone to Enzo Ferrari after Wigram, and Enzo, who was well pleased that Chris had beaten Jimmy and Lotus twice, asked what he needed. Chris got on the phone and said he needed another 15 horsepower. Mr Ferrari apparently said he'd see what he could do.

At Wigram the Lotus turned up for the first time in Gold Leaf livery — the dawning of the professionally sponsored racing team. The Ford horsepower told, Clark and Chris running 1-2 throughout, with Clark winning by 7.7 seconds.

Bruce McLaren was driving for BRM and described the spirit of the series in his *Autosport* column:

After Pukekohe we spent a few days at Lake Taupo water-skiing, swimming and (unsuccessfully) fishing. We've had a few barbecues too, but none to beat the spread put on by Chris Amon's mother and father at their beach house. The stack of steaks and sausages waiting for the barbecue was just fantastic — it would have fed an army. I counted 50 people there, and after the cricket match on the lawn in the afternoon, they made a fair-sized hole in the food.

The 'Kiwis vs Poms' cricket match is now an annual event, but thanks to Tim and Virginia Parnell, the Kiwis never seem to win. Virginia keeps the score, and Tim gets in front of the wicket (three fruit boxes, one on top of the other) so that you've virtually got to knock him down to hit the wicket. Frank Gardner tried it several times, but it's a bit difficult trying to fell a bloke the size of Big Tim with a tennis ball! Anyway, our side lost — again.

It's good to see Chris Amon doing so well in the Ferrari out here, and considering that he's looking after the project on his own with only one junior engineer from the Italian factory, Roger Bailey from England, Bruce Wilson from New Zealand and Bill Bryce as his road manager, he's doing very well indeed. So far he's leading the series.

Probably to his own surprise, Bruce won the next round, at Teretonga, in the unwieldy BRM, with Clark and Chris second and fourth, both having gone off the road in separate incidents.

Wilson again:

It rained at Teretonga and Chris never got to start in the preliminary race. We were working in a tent in the paddock, and as we wheeled the Ferrari out, some well-meaning fellow lifted the tent fly shelter, which was heavy with rainwater, and it all poured down the trumpets and drowned the motor. Bruce had finally got the BRM V12 sorted out and he won at Teretonga. He'd been having fuel troubles and we had a talk about it. I solved the problem for him but copying a little trick I'd learned on the Ferrari. I don't think Chris was too pleased about me helping Bruce to beat him.

We went to Australia still leading the championship. The first race was at Surfers' Paradise, and Marelli had a surprise for Chris. There was a crate with a lovely little 4-valve version of the 2.4-litre

Dino V6 — with an extra 15 horsepower. The engine we'd been using was a 3-valver. We won the preliminary race easily because of the arguments about whether Jimmy could start with his cigarette sponsorship on the Lotus, and he was kept in the paddock. We realised that the new engine had an overheating problem in the prelim and it only did about 15 laps in the main race, but while it was running Chris said it was fantastic.

The next race was at Warwick Farm, in Sydney, and Chris said he wasn't interested in racing the 3-valve engine again. Marelli protested that they only had the one four-valver and it was overheating. It was a very special unit, he said, and we couldn't touch it. In fact Chris raced with the 'old' engine at Warwick Farm but convinced Marelli that I could help him dismantle the new engine to check the overheating problem. We rebuilt it in three days, in time for Chris to use at Sandown Park in what was to be one of the best races I ever saw him drive. The problem was caused by a shaving of aluminium dragged from a stud thread when they were putting the head on originally. This had found its way over a sealing ring and caused the overheating.

Chris was competitive again with the 4-valve engine and he took the fight to Clark in a race-long battle that saw them cross the finishing line with Chris level with the back end of the Ford-Lotus. Clark was looking across to see where Chris was in that final dash to the flag. It was the last Grand Prix he would win.

For Chris, finishing second just a tenth of a second behind Clark was of great personal satisfaction, because Clark was his yardstick. Six weeks later Clark was dead, killed in a Formula Two race at Hockenheim when he punctured a tyre and hit a tree. The motor-racing world was devastated in the way it would be when Ayrton Senna was killed at Imola in 1994.

Chris's own thoughts:

I don't think Jimmy's death slowed anybody down but I think it probably cast some doubts in people's minds. A lot of us had a sort of bullet-proof attitude at the time, and it certainly put a dent in that.

In terms of Jimmy as a driver, I was alongside him when he took the flag in the last race he ever won but he was the only guy that I really felt I could never beat. He always seemed to have so much left within himself. On my day I felt I could foot it with anybody else, but I never felt that Jimmy had to try that hard.

As a person I always compare him with Bruce [McLaren]. I hardly ever heard either of them say a bad word about anybody. You could try and provoke Bruce into saying something about someone but he just wouldn't. Jimmy was exactly the same. I think the only guy he ever criticised was himself.

He enjoyed himself in the Tasman Series, really getting into the spirit of things when he could relax his guard a bit. He didn't have the pressures that he had in Europe and he certainly did things down here that he didn't do anywhere else. But for all that, he had started to make mistakes in his last months. He lost it on the straight at Teretonga, and at Surfers' Paradise he threw it down the road and I led for a few laps. He had been going through that business of tax exile and living in Paris, and while he was more relaxed on the social side, I actually thought he was almost losing interest a bit in his racing.

Everyone who races has a feeling of immortality — that it's never going to happen to *you* — because if you didn't, you wouldn't do it. Jimmy's death was the most profound thing that happened to me in my racing career because I felt if it could happen to him, what chance did the rest of us have? When he was killed, it touched people who had no interest in motor racing. It got to an awful lot of people. That was the uniqueness of the guy. He was someone very special.

I was in that race at Hockenheim and it was a terrible day. There was light rain falling and the spray tended to hang in the trees like fog. You couldn't see anything until you got to the stadium area each lap. I was closest to Jimmy on the track and yet I saw nothing of his accident. I didn't know he'd had one until after the race. I was aware that there was dirt on the road and some activity but it wasn't a place where you were liable to go off. It was a long gentle corner that was absolutely flat, wet or dry. The works Lotuses for Jimmy and Graham and my Ferrari were all on Firestone Formula Two tyres that had been made in the States, and they were extraordinarily uncompetitive in the wet. They were dry-weather tyres with grooves cut in them. We were well down in the field with Jimmy ahead, me in the middle and Graham behind, but out of sight of each other until we reached the stadium area.

Next time round Jimmy was still 100 metres in front of me, but what I didn't know at the time was that it wasn't Jimmy, it was Graham in the other Lotus. He had made a pit stop and come back out in exactly the same position as Jimmy had been ahead of me. When the race finished, I remember getting to the pits and people had tears in their eyes. It was my first indication that anything had happened. The word had spread very quickly.

The cause of Jimmy's accident was always a mystery to me. It was generally said that it was a tyre problem, but I spoke to an engineer who saw all four tyres some time later, after they had been taken off the car, and he said there were large flat spots on the left front and right rear tyres, indicative of heavy braking. The right front tyre had very light braking-type scuff marks, and the left rear similar but slightly more pronounced. The way those tyres were marked suggests to me the possibility of something breaking in the left rear suspension. There was also the fact that Jimmy's car had been rear-ended in a shunt soon after the start in the Formula Two race at Barcelona the previous weekend, and the team hadn't had time to go back to the factory, which could have created a situation beyond the control of the crew on the road without factory facilities.

In his 1997 book *Jim Clark*, Eric Dymock wrote:

Theories concerning Clark's accident ranged from freak gusts of wind to errant pedestrians, and [Derek] Bell's hypothesis about the misfiring engine, but the most likely explanation was the explosive decompression of a tyre, throwing the car off course, and sideways into the fatal tree.

Investigations showed that a tyre had lost pressure through a slow puncture, and although centrifugal force kept it in shape at speed in a straight line, side force in the gentle curve caused the beading to loosen from the rim, and drop into the well. Clark was experiencing difficulties on the slippery surface but even he could not keep control. There was no safety barrier.

Chris defends his theory about the suspension failure.

The sudden gust of wind I would discount totally. It wasn't that sort of day. The reason the visibility was so poor was because the spray was hanging in the air because there was no wind. Derek's theory about a misfire? I didn't know about that, but if he was experiencing a misfire, why wasn't I catching him? And if he had a slow puncture and the tyre was being held up by centrifugal force on the straight, having just been through the slower corners in the stadium area only a few seconds before, surely he would have noticed it? Further, I have a great deal of difficulty reconciling 'explosive decompression' with 'a slow puncture'.

Enzo Ferrari's right-hand man, Franco Gozzi, recalls Clark's rear-ending crash that previous weekend in Spain in his book *Memoirs of Ferrari's Lieutenant*. Ickx, in the Dino, hit Clark on the second lap, putting him out of the race with a puncture and damaged rear suspension. 'I remember with how much determination Clark came to our pits,' wrote Gozzi.

'Tell your driver to calm down,' he growled furiously, 'because driving like that we'll all get hurt.' He was right and I asked him to accept our apologies, adding, to conserve a little dignity, 'But you English are all the same, you get stuck in, too, but when something happens to you, you get tough.' He became even more annoyed. 'I am not English, I am Scottish,' he replied icily, 'and don't you forget it.'

Chris again:

Ickx's Ferrari had apparently been fitted with new brake pads at the start and these hadn't bedded in. I wonder if that accident in Barcelona somehow contributed to a breakage? But we'll never know for sure and it won't bring Jimmy back.

That was the start of that terrible 7th of the month thing. First Jimmy on April 7th, then Mike Spence at Indianapolis on May 7th, Scarfiotti in a hill climb on June 8th, Jo Schlesser in the Honda at Rouen on July 7th. You started to think that the 7th of the month wasn't a helluva good day to be in a racing car.

At the end of the 1968 season, *Autocourse* rated Amon as number four in the world behind Jackie Stewart, Jochen Rindt and Graham Hill. 'If things had gone the other way for me, I could have won the world championship that year. As it turned out, I never even won a race,' Chris recalls ruefully.

In 1968 the brilliant young Belgian Jacky Ickx had joined Ferrari as Chris's team-mate. When Ickx drove for Wyer's endurance team, his total dedication didn't endear him to team-mates Hailwood and Hobbs, but Chris never had a problem. 'He was very much the number two. It was his first full year in Formula One, and apart from the fact that he was bloody quick in the rain and won in France, he was never on the pace with me. He was a very quiet, relaxed, easy-going guy. I never had a problem with him.'

Chris was in pole position in Spain, Belgium and Holland, and in the front row for the British, German, Italian, Canadian and Mexican Grands Prix. With massive understatement, he muses:

> I was a bit unlucky in leading races and pulling out with stupid things like a stone through the radiator or the petrol pump breaking, and then there was the gearbox breaking in Canada when I was a minute in the lead. If I had finished all the races I was leading, I would have won the championship in '68. There were also three wet Grands Prix and I never liked that car in the rain — I never liked racing in the rain anyway.

In the Spanish Grand Prix Chris was a clear leader over Graham Hill's Lotus for more than half the race but the Ferrari fuel pump quit after 58 laps and he was out. Then Ferrari stayed away from Monaco. 'I never quite understood why — to do with Bandini's death the previous year, I suppose,' says Chris. He told Alan Henry: 'I went as a spectator, stayed on a boat with Charles Lucas, got into a lot of trouble, got pissed and fell into the harbour. Ken Tyrrell offered me the Matra, but Ferrari wouldn't let me drive it. Servoz-Gavin led the race in it before whacking a guardrail.' He felt the Ferrari would have been very competitive at Monaco.

Chris excelled on the original, super-fast Spa circuit, a track for which he would eventually hold the Formula One lap record of 152 mph in perpetuity when the circuit was abandoned and replaced by a shorter, more sanitised version after Jackie Stewart suffered a high-speed crash at Spa in 1966 and campaigned for more safety in Formula One.

Chris had his own views on safety in racing. As he explained to Nigel Roebuck:

> There are people in this business who worry me. At Grand Prix Drivers' Association safety meetings they'd shout about cutting trees down, flattening banks and erecting guardrail all over the place. I'm surprised some of them didn't ask for guardrail in their hotel rooms. After all, most people die in bed.
>
> OK, fine, then you'd get into a race with some of these crusaders, and find they'd happily put you *over* their precious guardrails without giving it a thought.
>
> So long as I was in a car I trusted, I never worried too much about the track. It was up to me to keep out of the trees. When I started, going off the road meant hitting a telegraph pole or a house or something. And it meant that for the other guy, too. So respect for each other — common sense, really — was essential, and that stayed with me. Hearing some of these people screaming for run-off areas and catch-fencing and stuff gave the impression they intended to use it before the weekend was over.

At Spa Chris took pole position convincingly and led comfortably, but a sliver of stone punctured his oil radiator and he was out of the lead after only eight laps. His Ferrari had appeared for practice with a small hydraulically operated rear wing above the gearbox, signalling the start of a rush for aerodynamics. Chris wishes they hadn't bothered.

Our Ferrari was probably the best-handling car that season, but when we introduced the wing at Spa we were suddenly left behind.

I was on pole by nearly *four seconds* over Jackie in the Matra. I did that time with the little wing but I also did exactly the same time *without* the wing. What you gained round the corners was minimal because it was only a piddly little wing. We elected to run the wing in the race although timewise there was nothing in it, but everyone put the 4-second advantage down to the wing, which wasn't the case at all.

At Zandvoort for the Dutch Grand Prix, Chris was on pole for the third time that season but the race was wet and Ferrari made the wrong tyre choice. He finished a dismal sixth, hating the rain and fed up with the tyre decision, which had been beyond his control. It rained again in the French Grand Prix at Rouen, and once again the Ferrari tyre choice cost him dearly. They started Ickx on wets and Chris on dries. Ickx won the race and Chris was an unhappy 10th.

The British Grand Prix was at Brands Hatch, and the Lotuses, now sporting tall wings, were fastest in practice. Chris's Ferrari was on the outside of the front row. It was his 25th birthday.

Colin Chapman had quickly hitched on to the wing development and came up with these bloody great wings and stuck them on the suspension, which Ferrari would *never* do, and on a bumpy track like Brands Hatch the Lotus had miles more down-force than we did. I was the only one who could vaguely run with the three Lotus 49s.

We shot ourselves in the foot, really. If we'd stayed wingless, everyone would have stayed wingless and I probably would have led more races. The Lotus really wasn't a very good car until it got the wing, and while the Cosworth DFV engine was quite difficult in 1967 when it first came out — it gave either nothing or the whole lot at once — it was better in 1968. They just had *so* much power.

The two works Lotus-Ford 49s failed, but Jo Siffert came through with the Rob Walker Lotus. Chris gave his best but finished 4.4 seconds back in second place. It was a disappointment but it was also to be his best placing of the season.

Rob Walker remembered the scene in his pit when Siffert was leading in the blue Lotus 49 with the distinctive white Walker noseband, just yards ahead of the Ferrari.

I tried to concentrate exclusively on my timekeeping and giving Seppi accurate signals, and as I did so I was reassured to note that every time Chris put in a really quick lap and closed the gap by a fraction of a second, Seppi would put in a slightly quicker one and open it up again. I first began to think we might win when Forghieri showed Chris the 'Give all' signal. God knows what he thought Chris had been doing until then. Then Seppi began to pull away slightly as the Ferrari's tyres started to go off.

Much later, when the euphoria of our win was beginning to wear off, I remembered that race day had been Chris's birthday. I had walked with him before the start and had wished him luck and said I hoped he would give himself a really super birthday present by winning the race. Little did I know then that less than two hours later I would be hoping and praying that he would finish second.

For the German Grand Prix, on the old Nürburgring, Ickx and Chris dominated dry practice, but the weather was appalling on race day and Chris was off the road in the 12th lap. The Ferrari was fitted with a cockpit safety harness for the first time, mainly, Chris stresses, to hold him in over the high-speed brows of the old mountain course, which lifted the cars clear of the road several times a lap. 'It was bloody hard to stay in the seat; you'd lose grip of everything over the brows and you were hanging on to the wheel for dear life.' Actual crash safety seemed to be a secondary consideration, but the harness certainly paid off in this regard in the next Grand Prix, at Monza, Ferrari's home turf.

Chris started in the front row and was in the leading, slipstreaming group when the hydraulic pump activating the rear wing failed and fluid was pumped on to a rear tyre.

You could work the wing manually, or, when you put the brakes on, the wing used to tilt down. This was driven off the engine oil pump, and someone had neglected to do a union up properly. I was probably doing close to 200 miles an hour, and as I got on the brakes, the thing literally squirted oil on a rear tyre and the car swapped ends. It went backwards down the road into the guardrail, which folded back because I think the posts were fairly rotten. The guardrail launched me, and I ended up doing a quadruple somersault through the tops of the trees and, amazingly, landed the right way up, in a spectator area. The ironical thing about it all was that I had a couple of bruises on my shoulders from the seat belts but nothing else at all. If we hadn't fitted the seat belts those few weeks before — well, it doesn't bear thinking about.

The car hit a Shell advertising hoarding 30 or 40 feet in the air and then hit a tree, which deflected it to the right. I'd come off going into the first Lesmo corner and I proceeded down to the second Lesmo somersaulting through the tops of the trees parallel to the track.

There was a marvellous photo of the Ferrari completely upside down with me hanging on to the wheel about 40 feet in the air. If you turned the photo upside down it looked like a normal shot.

I had no idea where I'd ended up, but I undid the seat belts and climbed out and there were all these spectators crowding around asking if I was OK. I've still got this vivid memory of John Surtees, in his white helmet with a blue stripe, peering over the top of the guardrail about 30 feet above me. He said, 'Jesus! Are you all right?' He'd come off on my oil in the middle of my accident.

I was reasonably well known in Italy but John had won the world championship for Ferrari and was a hero. He clambered down the bank and a spectator *insisted* on giving him his MV-Agusta so that we could ride it back to the pits.

Chris started the Canadian Grand Prix, at Sainte Jovite, in the middle of the front row. As *Motor Racing* related:

Denny Hulme won the race for McLaren but the day really belonged to Chris Amon, who drove perhaps the finest race of his career. After setting equal fastest time in practice he kept his Ferrari in the lead from the first to the 72nd lap, despite losing his clutch on lap 8. The young New Zealander, who must go down as this season's unluckiest GP pilot, shared a new lap record at 1min 35.1sec and had built up a lead of more than a minute over his nearest rival when, with only 18 laps to go, his overstrained transmission finally let him down. That he did so well, changing gear without his clutch for so many laps but giving no obvious signs of difficulty, was a tribute to his skill. But for a small piece missing from the steel ring behind the diaphragm spring of the Ferrari clutch, he would surely have got that first Grand Prix win at last.

The CanAm series was where the money was made in international motor racing towards the end of the '60s, and Chris had tasted success with the early McLarens. He persuaded Ferrari to make a purpose-built car after his modified endurance cars had proved short on sheer grunt and competitiveness in earlier seasons. The 612 CanAm Ferrari was the biggest, most powerful and fastest racing car the Italian Scuderia had ever built. It was also late, making its solo appearance in the last race of the series — the Stardust Grand Prix — on a track in the desert outside Las Vegas. Ferrari blamed delays by the German makers of the special head gaskets for the 6222 cc V12 engine, said to give 620 bhp at 7000 rpm.

The Americans were impressed. It was certainly the biggest Ferrari ever built, measuring nearly seven feet across the tail. There were fences and fins and a mid-mounted broad wing. The *Road & Track* reporter wrote: 'The 612's angry bellow was still the most distinctive sound at the track.' Lots of power, then, good acceleration and a top speed of 185 mph, but minor braking problems.

Chris qualified ninth when he would have liked to be third behind the two McLarens, but this reflected the lack of development and so much last-minute preparation. Not that this mattered a jot, and never mind the huge cost of the project and the creation of a special car for just one race.

Denny Hulme led away from the rolling start in his McLaren M8A, and behind him, trying to be second into the first turn, were Bruce McLaren, in another McLaren, and Mario Andretti, in a Lola T160. They came together, Bruce spun, and there were cars going off the road amid blinding dust trying to avoid each other. Chris took successful avoiding action, but in the sandstorm that was thrown up the big Ferrari's throttle slides were hopelessly clogged and he was one of only two drivers not to take the restart.

Eight thousands miles from Maranello to cover less than quarter of a mile. More Amon black magic.

8

From flying start to faltering finish: Ferrari runs out

In discussions during the summer of 1968 in Modena, Chris and Bill Bryce hatched a plan to set up in the United Kingdom aviation business. Chris had learned to fly while he was still at school, and he used a Piper Twin Commanche to commute around Europe.

It was a practical means of getting around Europe. I'd met a few of the people in the European Cessna headquarters in Brussels in 1967, and in 1968 they suggested that I might like a Cessna dealership in the UK. This coincided with Bill Bryce's arrival on the scene from New Zealand and he seemed the ideal man to set up and run the business. We combined our names and called the new set-up Brymon Aviation, reckoning we would be able to sell five or six aeroplanes a year.

Bryce recalls that Chris and he discussed the aviation venture in the Real Fini Hotel in Modena in 1968 and that they set up their Cessna dealership at Thruxton airfield, which was also established as a motor-racing circuit, using the old perimeter roads as at Silverstone and Goodwood.

We sold Chris's Twin Commanche and I started instruction for my private pilot's licence in August 1968. We sold three Cessna 150s to the Western Aero Club, owners of Thruxton, and the first aircraft Brymon Aviation owned was a Cessna 172. In November 1969 we moved to Fairoaks, near Woking, in Surrey, taking over the Fairoaks School of Flying.

Brymon had very successful years during 1971 and 1972 while Chris was racing with Matra, and we sold a considerable number of new and used aircraft. I could see flight training and aircraft sales as a fluctuating business so we invested in our first commercial aircraft — a Britten Norman Islander.

Chris's racing manager at this stage was Richard Burton, who had actually negotiated a lucrative Matra contract for him at the end of the 1969 season while he was still battling to get into the new March team. He would sign with the French team a year later, probably wishing he had taken his manager's advice and done so without delay.

Buoyed by the early success of his fledgling aviation business, Chris was keen to expand the multi-engine market on a larger scale, but Bryce said he was not all that keen — 'It was a very fragile market' — and felt that Burton was fanning the Amon enthusiasm.

When I didn't agree with the move, it was decided that Burton would buy my half share in the company, but I queried his low offer. He had assured me that the shares were not worth very much and that his offer was a generous one, so I made that offer back to him, and after consultation with his advisors the deal was struck for me to take over Brymon Aviation.

Bryce sold out of Brymon in 1983 and went home to New Zealand to set up Newman Airways, which would become Ansett.

Chris makes the observation now that Bill and he had 'different ambitions' — as Bryce himself had pointed out — and 'when there was a requirement to sign personal guarantees for million-dollar aircraft purchases, I probably started to lose interest and Bill bought me out'.

The 1969 Tasman Series promised better fortune, and this time Chris took two of the Dino Ferraris south, with Derek Bell as his team-mate. Once again Bruce Wilson worked with the Amon Ferraris. 'This year we had 4-valve engines for both cars, and our competition came from Graham Hill and Jochen Rindt in the Lotuses, Frank Gardner in an Alfa Romeo-engined Mildren and Piers Courage in a winged Williams-entered Brabham-Cosworth.'

Chris started as successfully as he had the previous season, winning the New Zealand Grand Prix at Pukekohe and then the Levin race the following weekend. At Wigram, he was third behind Rindt and Hill but still led the series. Courage won at Teretonga with Chris, having led initially, third.

As Wilson recalls: 'Chris was in a class of his own winning the first two races as he had done the previous season, but Rindt got his revenge at Wigram.'

Across the Tasman, Chris won the Lakeside race in Queensland with team-mate Bell backing him up in second place.

Wilson again: 'We had been experimenting with a wing that could be adjusted from the cockpit. We worked it all out, fitting a jury-rigged wing on the roof of a Falcon pick-up truck. The Ferrari had heavier springs now and we fitted the wing, which electronically controlled from a solenoid operated by a button on the steering wheel. That was a first for electronic controls on the steering wheel.'

In a 2002 interview with Mark Hughes in *Motor Sport*, Chris recalled:

Our Tasman wing was activated by a Triumph 2000 overdrive solenoid unit: when you let go of the button, the wing stayed down; when you pushed the button, it came up. It worked really well. Not only did it give us better straight-line speed, but it gave the rear tyres an easier time. Before that the wheels were going into camber all the way down the straights. This put a stop to that.

Lakeside was a walkover, but at Warwick Farm Chris was eliminated in a first-lap accident in the rain when Courage spun in front of him. Chris and Courage were the only two who could win the Tasman title, and this accident effectively decided that Chris Amon was the 1969 Tasman Champion. He was a worthy winner. For the first time he had been able to prove his point: that in equal equipment he had the talent to win. But it was a point with which he would defeat himself in 1970, for with Chris Amon, making a point was often a good deal more important than making sense.

Says Wilson:

Jochen Rindt had won at Warwick Farm in the Lotus, and they were set for a battle royal at Sandown Park. Mindful of his race-long battle with Clark's Lotus the previous year, I suggested that Chris used a few extra revs, and those couple of hundred extra revs made all the difference. Chris took the lead from Rindt on the opening lap and never looked like being headed. He won easily and set a new lap record.

Chris remembers that race:

Before Sandown Bruce [Wilson] and I had discussed increasing the revs. We were running to about 8600 rpm, but in Formula Two, with the same valve gear, they were revving to about 10,000 rpm, so we went for a lower gear ratio and decided to rev it to 9600 rpm. I remember pulling out of Jochen's slipstream early in the race and just driving by him on the way to winning. I also remember the look of sheer surprise on his face. You could see it quite clearly because of his open-face helmet. Jochen's style was much more aggressive than Jimmy's, but the end result was pretty similar in terms of lap time. I reckon I was somewhere in between on style.

Wilson continues:

It was interesting from my point of view to be able to compare Chris and Derek [Bell], since they were in identical cars. After the Grand Prix at Pukekohe, where it had won, Chris's Ferrari was just about spotless. Derek had come in fourth, a lap behind, but his car had used more oil and about 4 litres more petrol. His brake pads were completely gone and his car was covered in brake dust. Chris had such a good *feel* for a car.

Chris was looking forward to the challenge of Formula One, confident after winning his Tasman title, but he went straight back into engine problems. 'We basically had a sports-car engine for the first Grand Prix of the 1969 season, at Kyalami. We used to rev it to 11-and-a-bit. Ferrari had decided that the Cosworth had more torque than we did, so they'd rev it less and fatten up the torque curve, but the thing was just bloody *hopeless*.'

Chris qualified beside Stewart in the Matra, a tenth of a second slower, in the second row of the grid, and spent much of the race embroiled with Rindt's Lotus, but the Ferrari bearings failed just before half distance and he was out.

'When I got back to Italy I had a meeting with the Old Man and told him that we needed to rev the things *more*, not bloody less, and I remember him asking for an engine for Barcelona that revved to 12,000 rpm. I told him I didn't *care* whether it was cammy.'

On the Monjuich Park circuit, on the hill above Barcelona, Chris qualified in the middle of the front row with Hill and Rindt either side in their high-winged Lotus 49s. This was the race that resulted in wings being banned. The wing struts crumpled on both Lotuses and Hill and then Rindt crashed heavily, leaving Chris with a clear lead. By half distance he was 40 seconds ahead of Stewart in the Tyrrell Matra-Ford. 'I was leading by a country mile when it blew apart. I think it was always going to blow apart. I just couldn't take a trick.'

At Monaco, where wings were banned after the first day of practice, Chris remembers starting the race with 249 litres of fuel on board.

They had to build a special extra tank over my knees to get enough fuel in. They'd really lost the plot by then. I was sitting in most of the fuel, and with the tank over my knees there was a huge amount of weight on the front wheels. You had a big steering wheel and obviously no power steering or anything like the modern guys have. All the oil and water ran through tubes beside you, so you were sitting in extreme temperatures the whole time. You could lose anything up to eight or 10 kilos' body-weight in a race and you inevitably developed arms and shoulders like a gorilla. It was very physical.

When I visited the Goodwood Festival a few years ago, they let me try Damon Hill's Williams for size and I was sitting in this lovely carbon-fibre set-up, all insulated so that no heat got into the cockpit. In my day you used to step out of the car at the end of a race as a sweaty, dirty mess, but now they get out of the car at the end of a race and they look as though they've just strolled round the block. I think the cars are far too clinical these days. A lot of the driving has been taken away from the driver. When I was racing, it was very easy to overrev the engine if you missed a gear change, but everything's controlled for the driver now and you can't overrev the engine. The gear change is flicking a little paddle on the steering wheel, and you just keep flicking it until you run out of gears, and then you flick it back when you want to change down. I suppose in my day, particularly in the late '60s and early '70s, the driver was probably 60 or 70 per cent and the car was the rest. I would venture to say that it's probably 20 per cent driver and 80 per cent car now — and that's a shame, I think.

For all the fuel and extra weight, Chris qualified on the 2-2-2 grid at Monaco beside Jackie Stewart, just 0.04 of a second slower, and ran second in the race until stopped with a broken differential after 17 laps.

The flat-12 Formula One engine was the same design of cylinder head, valves and pistons as on the V12 but laid flat. The first day I drove it at the Modena Autodrome it was 15 kph faster than the V12 car had been. It was just a different deal. The fact that it broke the crankshaft and blew up on the fourth lap was something else, but the sole reason for all the problems on the V12 was the oil-scavenging side of things. That was where Keith Duckworth was so clever with the Cosworth DFV V8, because he was the first designer who got an engine running with negative crankcase pressures. Duckworth was a brilliant guy and that's why his engine went so well.

When Ferrari went to the flat-12 configuration, the engine scavenged a lot better but it had an air-oil separator pump on it by this time and it made a huge difference. At Modena with the V12 we used to do one warm-up lap and one hard lap and the oil used to be up around 110°C. With the flat-12 it used to run at around 85–90°C. With the V12 there was so much oil that the crank was beating it around and heating it up.

The horsepower figures on the test bench weren't too bad and I had countless arguments with the Ferrari engine guys, who insisted they had the power and that it compared with a DFV they had got hold of to run on the bench. But once you put the V12 in the car and started accelerating and decelerating and putting lateral Gs on it, it wouldn't scavenge. It took a long time to convince them.

These turbulent tests with the new flat-12 prompted Chris to contemplate making a move.

It was mainly out of frustration. I was testing the new engine in the August of 1969, and while it was clearly a lot quicker than the V12, we were only doing perhaps three or four laps and it would break a crankshaft or have a major failure. I really felt that the 1970 season had the potential to be exactly the same as 1969, and I didn't need that.

I considered my two main rivals at that time: Jackie Stewart and Jochen Rindt. They were both using the Ford-Cosworth DFV V8, and I was very keen to have the same power package behind me. Robin Herd had been a designer at McLaren in the early days and he was now involved with the March set-up, and he approached me in the middle of 1969 to tell me that they were building a Formula One car. He approached me again in September, when I had already signed a 1970 contract with Ferrari, but the new car had failed so many times that I went to see Enzo Ferrari and told him I wanted out. We agreed to disagree and I signed with March.

The Ferrari 612 CanAm car had been dusted-off, now with a claimed 660 bhp at 8000 rpm, and was entered for Chris to drive at Watkins Glen in July, where he finished third behind Bruce McLaren and Denny Hulme in their McLaren-Chevrolets, 23 seconds adrift. It was another personal project, similar to his Tasman entry: Ferrari supplied the machinery and spares and he did the rest. Weight was allegedly trimmed by 1600 lbs since the car's brief Las Vegas debut the previous season, a smaller body had been designed and the suspension had been comprehensively modified. A wing was being designed in California.

In the next round, at Edmonton, Alberta, Chris was finally annoying the McLarens, and although it was said by all concerned that they were 'making a race of it' and letting the Ferrari lead for a while, Bruce's car swallowed a piston and it was a different Kiwi CanAm 1-2: Hulme and Amon. Chris was just five seconds adrift. The *Autosport* headline was apt: 'DENNY SEES RED'.

At Mid-Ohio there was a Ferrari engine problem in practice and Chris started midgrid. As *Road & Track* told it: 'For nine laps it was a great race, Amon taking that long to move from 13th to third, despite the fact that his "good engine" had gone to pieces the day before.' Bruce suffered an oil-pump seizure and only just made the finish but was still second, 50 seconds behind Denny and a lap ahead of Chris. But the Ferrari delivered something of a signal when Chris claimed the fastest lap at 1 minute 29.1 seconds (an average speed of exactly 100 mph).

Come Elkhart Lake the Ferrari had a McLaren-sized rear wing from Lamar in California, and Chris reported to Bill Gavin that he could now throw the car around. Overheating and a cracked chassis tube during qualifying put Chris down in seventh spot, but once the race started he was instantly up to third and again the three Kiwis played with the lead at the head of the field. Bruce and Denny pulled away together, then eased back late in the race, by which time Chris was out of it, coming home a comfortable third after his fuel pump had failed with only seven laps left.

Bridgehampton saw more engine changes for the Ferrari, and the Italian general strike that had been harming the Formula One programme during the summer was also hurting Amon's fledgling CanAm project. Pete Lyons wrote in *Autosport*: 'It hardly seems to matter what comes from Italy any more, as they tear the engine apart upon arrival and rebuild it themselves as a matter of course anyway. Additionally, Bill Gavin says he is interested to find that what in fact the CanAm team seems to be doing is running a development programme for the 512 Group 4 car — "at our expense, and you may quote me."'

Chris qualified third fastest behind Bruce and Denny and ahead of John Surtees in another McLaren. There were Ferrari problems the night before the race, and Lyons reported: 'Roger Bailey was swimming in oil under the Ferrari, feeling through the sump drainings for bearing fragments: he found nothing, but as a precaution all the bearings were renewed anyway.' Chris was lying fourth on the third lap when he saw his oil pressure plummet and switched off, fearing a broken con rod.

At Michigan the engine again failed in practice and the Amon team withdrew. In qualifying for the Laguna Seca round the final Ferrari engine quit on race morning, and in a last-minute scramble Chris accepted a ride in the third McLaren. He was allowed just three laps of special practice in the M8B and started from the back of the grid.

Lyons again:

Roger Bailey and his cohorts have to improvise massively. The crankshaft throw damaged in practice at Michigan was ground down 30 thou and chrome plated. The Ferrari bearings were replaced with — sssh, big secret — Chevrolet shells. During Friday practice the chrome ripped right off in a wad. In a long sleepless session the engine was removed again — the entire operation to remove-and-replace involves crow-bars to get the mounts to line up and can take 10 hours — and the offending journal ground down another 10 thou. But it was all to no avail: during the Sunday warm-up sessions the oil pressure dropped once again. This time the cog belt to the oil pump was the culprit, and now the mechanics are considering they may have been misleading themselves all along thinking the bearings were the prime fault.

Denny and Bruce roared away in the lead. By lap 14 Chris was eighth, closing in on Jo Siffert's Porsche — 'Seppi wasn't actually helping me get by' — who threw up a tyre marker that smashed the nose of Chris's McLaren. He pitted for a replacement, losing a lap and dropping back to 13th. With nine laps left, he eventually retired with a differential problem. After the race, he told Lyons he was interested to see that after three years he and Bruce still had different ideas about setting up a racing car. In 1966 he had found that the early M1C McLarens had oversteered too much for his personal taste, and the M8B he had driven at Laguna Seca, as set up by Bruce, also oversteered too much.

Chris's CanAm Ferrari venture had netted a total of 39 points for sixth place in the championship. It had also earned a total of $47,200 prize money. Bruce McLaren had won the championship and $160,960.

It took Ferrari more than half the 1970 season to establish some sort of reliability and start finishing races in Formula One, but Chris had misgivings about his decision to walk out.

I actually regretted leaving Ferrari, not from the results point of view but from the fact that I suddenly thought, "What the hell have I done, leaving a team like that?" But there had been a lot of pressure in 1969 because we weren't getting results and I was getting a hard time from the Italian press. The team was generally very unhappy because of all the peripheral things that were going on. Maybe it was a bit of a kneejerk reaction — it's certainly a decision that I have regretted since.

Enzo Ferrari was never a man to accept being snubbed. Chris Amon did it and John Surtees had done it. As Ferrari wrote in his memoirs:

Chris Amon was the Nazarro of the sixties. But he lacked the sincere human warmth of that unforgettable artist of the steering wheel. In the three years he drove for Ferrari he never achieved the success he deserved. He was a good, indeed an excellent test driver, unfussy and intuitive, but on the racetrack he didn't have what it takes and his strength often seemed to run out when it was needed. After his time at Ferrari he drifted from team to team in a vain attempt to overcome the adversities that he was constantly encountering. In the end he went back to his native New Zealand and devoted himself to his family. I wonder if his children believed him when he told them how very near he had been to becoming a motor-racing legend.

I confess I don't understand the comparison with Felice Nazarro. The only major link I can find between Ferrari and Nazarro is that Nazarro won the first race the 10-year-old Enzo saw when his father took him and his brother Alfredo to watch the Circuito di Bologna in September 1908. Chris feels Ferrari penned the piece in a moment of pique. 'It was probably to do with the fact that I'd agreed to drive for him in 1970 and then changed my mind. He was actually very keen to get me back into the team in 1973.'

Years later Chris read a newspaper quote from Nigel Mansell likening being offered a drive for Ferrari to getting a call from the Vatican to visit the Pope. 'I don't think it was the same thing at all. There have been a lot of popes and there will be many more in the future — but there will be only *one* Enzo Ferrari.'

9

Dreams and nightmares: March, Indy and Bruce's death

Chris had signed to drive a March 701, a car that is generally seen in retrospect as sturdy and workmanlike rather than inspired, the first off-the-peg Formula One car built down to a price rather than up to whatever it took. 'March' was an acronym of the initials of the team principals — Max Mosley, later to become the ultimate head of Formula One as president of the Fédération International de l'Automobile (FIA), Alan Rees, Graham Coaker and Robin Herd. The company was built on dreams: there were those who said the name stood for 'Much Advertised Racing Car Hoax'. Chris was to get his Cosworth DFV but his contract seemed to change by the day.

> The whole March deal was totally misrepresented to me. The saga started in Barcelona in 1969, when I was having breakfast on the morning of the Spanish Grand Prix and Robin Herd joined me. He said he was putting together a team for next year and would I be interested in driving? I told him I knew about the team but that I thought it was supposed to be for Jochen. Herd said that Jochen wasn't going to be involved, that he would either retire or stay with Lotus. I told him to let me know more about it, but I never heard from him until September, when I was in the middle of the crankshaft problems with the new flat-12 Ferrari engine. The crankshafts seemed to be breaking every couple of laps in testing and the prospects didn't look bright.
>
> I had a meeting at a Heathrow hotel with Mosley and Herd and

they promised a one-car team built around me. As far as they were concerned it was a done deal. They said they had plenty of money and it all sounded fantastic as presented to me then, but in my opinion it was a complete con. Had I known what was going to happen, there is no way I would have got involved. The whole thing mushroomed and there would be *six* cars because they needed the finance — and yet they had told me that the finance was already in place. I feel particularly strongly about this. It was my own fault that I left Ferrari, but I left on the basis of a completely false premise. Would I have been better off letting Richard Burton do the deal? Absolutely.

Richard Burton could see the shortfalls in the March contract and had opened negotiations with the French Matra team, who were now without the talents of Jackie Stewart in the Tyrrell-entered Matra-Ford. A Matra link with Chrysler had ended the liaison with the Tyrrell team. Unbeknown to the world of Formula One, Burton had a Matra contract ready for Chris's signature on 19 November 1969, and had spotted a loophole that would let Chris out of his March deal.

'In fact the Matra offer was a tempting one, but if I went there I would be getting myself into another unknown quantity enginewise, although I knew that the Matra organisation was better than Ferrari's,' Chris told *Autosport* in February 1970.

The potential for success at Ferrari had been there, but there had been no success. They had the manpower but not the organisation to follow it through, and there was a continuous engine problem in all classes. I went there with the impression that Ferrari had the best engines and the worst chassis, but more often than not it was the other way round.

The Matra car looked impressive, and so did the team and the facilities, but I was worried about the engine. I finally decided that I wouldn't sign for them and that's why I left without driving the car.

The lure of the Ford-Cosworth engine was too much, and Chris put his signature to a March contract. Another of those things in his career that he would look back on and ruefully shake his head over.

Jackie Stewart, Francois Cevert, Jo Siffert, Mario Andretti and Ronnie Peterson all raced March 701s during the 1970 season. Chris must have had more cause to wonder at his decision to leave Ferrari. He had achieved his goal of getting a car with a Ford-Cosworth V8 engine to race against Stewart and Rindt, and his long-held desire to get a car the equal of Stewart's had been realised, but the vehicle fell short of the ideal he wished it to be. He fretted that all the results of his testing would eventually be passed on to the Tyrrell team as well as the other March customer team-owners. What had started out as a one-car dream-team was turning into a multi-car nightmare, and he was spending far too much time on team politics, fighting a move to have both Jo Siffert and Ronnie Peterson in works cars for the sponsorship they would bring the beleaguered Mosley.

There was a dividing line between the March-March and Tyrrell-March teams. The Amon works car was with Firestone, and Chris had a good working relationship with the American company and its engineers. Tyrrell was with Dunlop, so Chris's test results would not necessarily be transferable to Tyrrell's cars.

In fact, the first time Chris and Stewart lined up against each other, for the South African Grand Prix at Kyalami, in March, they had set identical qualifying times. Stewart had set the time first so was on pole for what was the season's opener, Chris was beside him in the middle of the front row, and Brabham was on the outside in his Brabham-Ford.

I wrote in my *Autocar* column the following week:

I heard someone say that there were two Marches on the front row of the grid at Kyalami because of the drivers. If one hadn't been Stewart and the other hadn't been Amon trying to pip Stewart or at least demonstrate that he was able to stay with the champ, the Marches might have been further back. This reliance on the driver rather than the machine comes out in a *Motor Trend* interview with Roger Penske in America when he was defending his switch from GM Chevrolet to the American Motors Javelin in TransAm racing: 'I happen to think that racing is like other sports. In golf it doesn't matter what kind of club Nicklaus swings or what kind of ski Killy uses. What happens really depends on the guy swinging the club or going down the slopes. If all the cars are equal then the same thing applies.' Roger was talking TransAm, but his words probably apply to formula 1 as well, since the 3-litre Ford-Cosworth V8 seems to be the great equaliser these days.

Rindt came off the second row to try to split Chris and Brabham but succeeded only in knocking both down the field and his own Lotus spinning off the track, while Stewart sped off in the lead. Brabham recovered and came through to win, while Chris was out with overheating after 14 laps, a weld having broken in the cooling system.

It was a small failure, but in the Amon way of seeing things early in 1970 it was massively symbolic. The atmosphere was tense. That season, journalist Ted Simon wrote a book, *The Chequered Year*, chronicling the fortunes of the new March team. He was a general features writer rather than a dedicated motor-sports journalist, so he wrote as he saw, and he saw Chris Amon as a complicated, highly strung personality rather than the casual laid-back man I usually saw.

Temperamentally, Chris is a distinct outsider among the very best drivers. His urge to drive seems to come from a different quarter and the satisfaction he derives fulfils a different need. The others sense this in him, a quality they don't understand and can only explain to themselves as weakness. According to their different natures, they are sympathetic, indifferent or contemptuous of the way Chris's unusual character expresses itself.

Speculation was rife as to whether the new March cars performed better with or without their distinctive side 'pod' fuel tanks. I asked Ken Tyrrell whether the side tanks really did provide additional down-force and were an improvement. 'Funny you should say that,' he said with a grin. 'Brabham's just been along and asked me the same question, and I told him it cost me £9000 to find the answer and I wasn't about to tell him.' The off-the-shelf March Formula One cars were available for £9000 complete less the Cosworth DFV V8 engine, which was now also available to customers at £7500.

The International Trophy race at Silverstone in April was for a mix of 3-litre Formula One and 5-litre Formula 5000 cars and run as two 26-lap heats with results according to aggregate time. Chris was in his element with his red works March winning the first heat, thereby notching up his very first win in Formula One, albeit only half of a nonchampionship race. Stewart recovered his pace in the second heat and led throughout in the blue Tyrrell-March, but Chris was on his tail, comfortable in the knowledge that he would win on aggregate if he finished within 12 seconds of Stewart. He finished second, just 2 seconds down on Stewart, which gave him overall victory with the fastest lap of 1 minute 22.1 seconds (an average speed of 128.35 mph).

The Spanish Grand Prix at Jarama, near Madrid, was a discouraging one for Chris. He started sixth, having qualified 0.05 of a second faster than his

Ferrari nemesis Jacky Ickx, who was gradually finding form in the new flat-12 Ferrari. His problems began before the start.

> The clutch wouldn't disengage properly, so when I got into gear I started cranking forward, just going, going, going, and I couldn't stop, so I had to push it out of gear, and then I tried pushing it in again and couldn't. So I was stuck there and all I could do was coast out of the way to the side. I had the engine off and the car in gear, so that when the flag dropped I pressed the starter button and jerked my way down the road until it started. I got away well back in last place and passed two cars before the engine went off song coming down the end of the straight at the end of the first lap.

He made three pit stops with a misfiring engine and finally quit on lap 10. He had a broken camshaft. Stewart won the race to give the unloved and unlovely March 701 its only Grand Prix victory. Tyrrell was already having a Formula One car of his own designed and built, and it would appear before the end of the season.

Chris had signed to drive at Indianapolis in a two-car works team of M15 McLaren-Offenhausers with Denny Hulme.

> When Bruce asked me to drive for him at Indy in 1970, it went a long way to re-establishing the bond I always felt had been broken when I left for Ferrari at the end of 1966, but the M15As weren't very good and had huge turbo lag
>
> I felt I had to have another go at Indy. It was a mistake. My dislike for the place in 1967 soon turned to a real hate for it in 1970. To start with, that first Indy McLaren wasn't a very good car and I don't think anybody who drove it really liked it, including Denny.
>
> Indianapolis really is a strange place, and one of the most

peculiar things about it is this groove thing. On the track there's a definite groove into which you have to get yourself. This is a very difficult thing to explain, but basically what it amounts to is that you can go round and round, and go slower and slower, and the harder you try, the slower you go, and for whatever reason I just wasn't able to find the groove as easily or as quickly as some of the other guys. I remember one day I did start to get it together, and it felt good; it was coming out of the corners nicely and I was turning in laps at around 165 mph.

This was during the week before Monaco, and after that session I told Bruce [McLaren] that I thought I'd got it all sorted out and that I was off to Monte Carlo. I ran 10 laps at 169–170 mph, which was right on the pace, and everyone was saying I'd cracked it. I felt happy with it too, and thought I'd finally mastered the thing. It all seemed plain sailing. I'd go back the following week and qualify for the race without any problem. Well, I did go back and I just couldn't get the bloody thing within five miles an hour of my speed the week before. I have absolutely no explanation for it. One of the old USAC guys told me I should be getting down as low on the track as I could. I told him if I got any lower I'd be running on the golf course. Jimmy Clark once told me that if he couldn't get up to a competitive speed one day, he would pack up and go back to the motel. Then, next day, everything would be fine. Incredible, isn't it? It really is an entirely different way of driving, and I never got along with it. You either tended to go well or not — there was no happy medium.

I remember Bobby Unser got in my McLaren and went four or five miles an hour faster, but when he got out of the car and lit a cigarette, his hands were shaking. He said, 'Well, it's not bad, but it's a little tricky in places.' I didn't like it *at all*.

One of the differences is that, unlike a Grand Prix race, you have to look way ahead of you all the time, rather than at your front wheels. I remember Mauri Rose [a three-time winner of the Indianapolis 500] telling me what he thought was the best way to get round the place: 'You imagine that it's a dark night, it's snowing, and you're trying to get to a house with some lights on, about 400 yards away. Now if you're trying to get to that house, you're going to look at the lights rather than the ground in front of you, and that's what you must do at Indianapolis. Look at where you want to finish up, not where you are at the moment.' His advice was absolutely right. Apart from anything else, speeds are so bloody high at Indy that you have to look way ahead so as not to get involved in somebody else's accident — you're on it before you can blink.

Now this is all very well, but Indy is very narrow, and the cars run very close together. If you're concentrating on what's happening 3–400 yards up the road, you're not watching who's running next to you. I'm convinced this is the reason for some of those inexplicable shunts at Indy, where a guy twitches around as if he's got the whole track to himself. Simply, you can't watch everything at the same time, and at 200 mph any kind of mistake can lead to a multiple shunt, such as the one at the beginning of the 1966 race. I saw the film of that race before I ever went to the place, and it had a big effect on me.

When I got back to Indy after Monaco that year [1970], it was just hopeless. I couldn't get on it at all, and then Denny had his bad accident in the other McLaren, baling out when it caught fire, and that really did it — I jacked it in once and for all and went back to Europe. Funnily enough, my next race was the Belgian Grand Prix at Spa, and I felt completely at ease straight away. Odd, isn't it? There are people who hate Spa and aren't at all bothered by Indy. I'm just the opposite. I remember Bruce saying that maybe they should paint trees on the walls at Indy and it would make me feel at home.

Monaco was more encouraging, and once again Stewart and Chris were fastest in qualifying in the Marches. Stewart led initially from Chris, before Brabham muscled through to put Chris in third. Then Chris was back up to second when Stewart's engine started misfiring and Brabham took the lead. He pitted after 27 laps with a misfire, and fell out after 61 laps when a bolt dropped out of the rear suspension and sent him into a wild spin.

The summer of 1970 was a traumatic one, with the deaths of Bruce McLaren on 2 June, Piers Courage 19 days later at Zandvoort, and Jochen Rindt during practice for the Italian Grand Prix at Monza in September.

I was driving back from the March factory on 2 June. It was a lovely afternoon and the Belgian Grand Prix was at Spa — a track that I liked — the following weekend. I was cruising through the Oxfordshire countryside and had the radio on when it came over the news. I stopped the car, got out and just stood there for a while. There are a few events that you always remember where you were and what you were doing when you heard about them, and that was definitely one of them. I'll never forget that day. I was numb. When things happen during a race your adrenaline is going and it takes over your mind. But when you're just driving along the road and you're not pumped up at all, it's stark reality.

While Chris had been driving for Ferrari and based in Italy, he hadn't seen all that much of Bruce, but as fate would have it,

I'd just spent the thick end of a month with Bruce at Indianapolis and that made it even more devastating for me. I'd just quit their

Indy programme a week before the race.

Suspension-mounted wings had been banned in 1969, and this would have been the first body-mounted wing on the McLaren CanAm car. The wings had previously been on struts, but for 1970 they had the same-sized rear wing mounted between tail fins that put huge stresses on the body-fixing pins at the forward edge. I'm not entirely sure that anyone in those days would have worked out how much down-force the wings were generating or how much stress was being put through those fastening pins. They were thumping great wings. They didn't have the underbody aerodynamics but they had those giant wings that were putting huge amounts of down-force, which literally lifted the lid — opened the rear body section. You could imagine the leverage of the wing at the back of the car and the body hinging back and located in the middle, just behind the cockpit — and all that down-force was trying to do was open the engine cover.

The Belgian Grand Prix was a sad occasion without the McLaren team, and the team people in the pit lane were missing Bruce, who had scored his first Grand Prix win in his own car at Spa two years earlier. Again Stewart and Chris were on the front row in the Marches, this time split by Rindt in the Lotus.

Chris was haunted by his seeming inability to win when he was always so close, and prone to bouts of angry depression — anger at himself and his lack of luck when he obviously had ability in abundance. Ted Simon wrote:

If Amon had looked like a temperamental man, if he had had the arrogance of Rindt or even the recklessness of Rodriguez, perhaps his moods would have been passed over without surprise. Chris was not the outdoor extrovert he appeared to be. He was deeply

∧
Not a car to fill one with confidence — McLaren's 1970 Indy 500 challenger, the M15.

∧
Possibly the last shot of New Zealand's 'trio at the top', taken at the 1970 Indy 500. Also pictured are Tyler Alexander, Teddy Mayer and Gordon Coppuck.

^
Leading the March: Chris rounds Eau Rouge ahead of similarly mounted Jackie Stewart during the 1970 Belgian Grand Prix.

^
Manhandling the ill-behaved March during the 1970 German Grand Prix.

∧
The three flying Kiwis at Brands Hatch for the 1970 Race of Champions.

∧
The unloved and unlovely Lotus 70 Ford F5000 in the 1971 New Zealand Grand Prix.

∧
Chris did a lot of testing at Matra. Here he drives the Matra-Simca sport prototype M660.

∧
Starting 16th on the grid at the Nürburgring, 1971.

∧

'The visor race.' Chris led from pole at Monza in 1971.

>

A holiday in Ibiza resulted in
a short-lived goatee, here on
display at Monza.

∧
Leading Emerson Fittipaldi's Lotus 72 at Jarama, in the 1972 Spanish Grand Prix.

∧
Running out of brakes at Monza while challenging for the lead.

^
Chris in his Matra in the 1972 Le Mans 24-hour race. His co-driver was Jean-Pierre Beltoise.

^
The 1973 'McCall' Tecno at Zolder.

∧
Chris Amon competing for Talon at Wigram.

∧
Driving with a painful wrist in Mo Nunn's underfunded Ensign at Monte Carlo, 1976.

concerned with himself, and troubled by his concern. Over the year he became more and more to seem like a man searching in himself for a flaw, or a broken part which could be repaired so that he might, at last, finish the race and win.

Reading that passage recently, Chris observed that Simon would have been totally unaware of the conflicts within the management of the team.

Chris led the opening lap and then traded the lead with Stewart during the laps that followed, demonstrating at last that he really could match the world's best in a Grand Prix with an equal car. Stewart retired with engine failure after 14 laps, and Pedro Rodriguez, who had shaken free from the pack in the BRM and come motoring up behind, took the lead with an ease that angered Chris. There was *no way* that the BRM could suddenly be that fast. There was *no way* that it could be that reliable. The final lap typified his career of ill fortune. He set the fastest time: 3 minutes 27.4 seconds (average speed 152.077 mph), a Formula One record that would stand for evermore, as the old original road course would be closed in 1973 (although parts of it would be used in the shorter modern track that eventually replaced it). That was faster than Stewart's pole time, which signalled the effort Chris was making either to take the lead or to break the 12-cylinder BRM by forcing the Mexican into a mistake. He finished 1.1 seconds behind, in second place, not so secretly convinced that the BRM's surprising turn of speed was due to the use of a 3.3-litre engine.

(To be strictly accurate, Chris holds the Formula One lap record for the circuit with a chicane at Malmedy. The outright lap record for the 'old Spa' was set by Henri Pescarolo, who drove 3 minutes 13.4 seconds (average speed 163.093 mph) in a Matra during the 1000-kilometre endurance race in 1973.)

At Zandvoort Chris started in the second row but was out after two laps with a fried clutch. Piers Courage was killed when his De Tomaso crashed in flames. The French Grand Prix was at Clermont Ferrand, and Chris and Stewart were together on the second row. Chris was well aware that Ickx was on pole with the Ferrari he had turned down, but he stayed in the race to finish second again, this time behind Rindt's Lotus 72, while Ickx went out with a broken engine.

The British Grand Prix was at Brands Hatch, and the bumpy track didn't favour the Marches. Stewart was down in sixth on the grid while Chris was as far back as 17th, although fought his way home in fifth. At Hockenheim he went out with a blown engine.

> The 701 was a very basic car and the only way you could make it go was to drive it on the throttle and slide it around a bit. I remember at Hockenheim, in the second qualifying session, giving the thing bloody heaps, coming round the corner on to the pit straight with the tail out in total oversteer. When I came in to the pits, Max [Mosley] bent down into the cockpit and said, 'Would you mind coming through that corner a little differently? It's making the car look bad.'
>
> In fact I had been able to hold the Ferraris and Rindt's Lotus at Hockenheim but I couldn't pass because I didn't have enough power. The slippery shape of the Lotus 72 was better than our March but I think that Lotus and Tyrrell also had better Cosworth engines than we did. Even so, on a fast circuit I was right with them.

In Austria Chris was eighth and a lap down. 'I'd been running quite well but I gradually drifted back through the field with a damper problem. Max announced to the press that the driver — me — had lost interest during the race, but Pete Kerr, one of my mechanics, announced in turn that one of my rear shock absorbers had lost all its oil.'

On a lighter side, Chris recalled dinner after the race in Germany at the same restaurant as the Ferrari mechanics. 'The wine was flowing and I got the Italians singing. They loved singing. They all reckoned they were potential Pavarottis, and in fact Pavarotti came from Modena. They were all in good voice that evening, and then Max Mosley surprised everyone with his rendition of *Lloyd George Knew My Father* — and of course he *did*!' Max's father, Oswald Mosley, was a controversial politician in prewar Britain.

Ickx had been second for Ferrari in Germany and scored his first win with the flat-12 in Austria. At Monza he started in pole position but the qualifying was overshadowed by Jochen Rindt's fatal crash on the Saturday afternoon. Chris was seventh, a lap down, but Stewart battled Regazzoni's Ferrari for the lead to eventually finish second in his last race in a March.

Jochen's death made a big impact on me because I knew him pretty well. I remember having dinner with him one night in London in midseason and he was saying he was sick of the racing and sick of the way of life. He said that he thought he had a chance of winning the title in 1970 and he would retire at the end of the year. Basically he wanted out. But then I remember talking to him a few weeks later and he was saying he was going to re-sign for another year.

It's fair to say that at that time Jackie, Jochen, Jack Brabham and I were extremely competitive. I considered those three my major rivals. Jochen was very quick and so was Jackie, but in a slightly different way. Jackie was a much more polished performer, but in terms of speed and race craft there probably wasn't much in it. Jack was older than us but he was right on the pace that season.

Jochen's death had the same shocking impact on the racing community as I'm sure Ayrton Senna's did 24 years later.

One of the questions I'm so often asked in relation to the number of drivers who died in that era is 'Why did you keep doing it?' It's a very hard question to answer. You had to proceed on that basis, and none of us had the benefit of hindsight. I guess it was an accepted part of motor racing in those days and we can thank God that it isn't now.

Looking back on it, you wonder how you planned your week. Or your year. Or your future. But we did.

I couldn't understand what had happened with us at Monza because the March wasn't a bad car on fast, smooth circuits and Monza was a track where I'd done thousands of test laps for Ferrari. I was on pole for Matra the following year but here I was with the 701 struggling to get on to the back of the grid. It didn't make sense, but then I remembered that when we were testing for six weeks at Kyalami, Cosworth had built a detuned engine that would do hundreds of miles without rebuilding so far from home. It was 2 seconds off the pace, but that was fine for testing. I strongly suspect that they gave me this engine at Monza to make it look as though I was underperforming.

They were meant to be paying me £100,000 for the season in four equal payments and we'd got to September and they had only made one payment, so there was the small matter of them hoping that I would maybe walk away from the deal at Monza, which would get them off the hook financially. They would have had a stronger case if I hadn't qualified for the race.

I don't see another way of explaining how I could qualify all season near the front of the grid, be so slow at Monza, and then run strongly again in the next Grand Prix in Canada. Why, on a relatively easy circuit that I knew very well, did I struggle to qualify? We never did sort out the financial side, but that was just an example of the politics and bullshit that went on that season.

In the Canadian Grand Prix Stewart started on pole in the new Tyrrell while Chris soldiered from back in sixth on the grid to third place. The Ferraris of Ickx and Regazzoni were first and second respectively. The irony of the situation was not lost on Chris, who was reaching the end of his tether with March. At Watkins Glen he started and finished fifth, and in the final race of the season, in Mexico, he started fifth again and finished fourth.

Unfortunately our March was about as good at the beginning of the season as it was ever going to be, and while I had some reasonable results it just didn't go on, and as the season went by we got less and less competitive. March was teetering on the edge of bankruptcy by the end of the season and I hadn't been paid for about three-quarters of it, so when Matra made me a very good offer it was an easy decision to make.

Jackie Stewart wrote of Chris's frustrations and outbursts during that summer of 1970 at March in his book *Faster — A Racer's Diary*:

Chris is a very open and relaxed guy who's great fun to be with, although sometimes he gets terribly tied up, particularly during practice. Anger can boil up inside him which you never suspected was there, and by now his mechanics have a fairly thorough description of it. They call it Chris's 'wobblies'. There are three kinds, each corresponding to the intensity of his mood: the white, the rainbow and the purple wobblies. The white variety is when he gets out of his car, his face ashen, throws his gloves down and simply screams 'Fucking car,' and storms off. The rainbow type is when he explodes at everything, makes no discriminations and is close to outright hysteria. The purple wobblies, the peak of his outbursts, set in when he's completely without measure, his face beet red, his blood pressure up, eyes bulging and he's almost wrenching everybody apart.

In fact it was not the end of the March 701 saga. Chris had agreed to drive for Andy Granatelli's STP team in the 1971 Tasman Series in the car that Mario Andretti had raced in Formula One, but fitted with experimental McNamara suspension and the 2.5-litre Tasman version of the 3-litre Ford-Cosworth Formula One engine. Andretti had driven the car to third place in the Spanish Grand Prix at Jarama, the race that Jackie Stewart had won to score the 701's only Grand Prix victory. 'That March wasn't a very good Formula One car and it *certainly* wasn't a good Tasman car with that 2.5 Cosworth. It was too heavy for Formula One and with the smaller engine it was just completely off the pace.'

The series started at Levin, Chris's home track, but he could do no better than a distant third. Granatelli had hoped for much better things from the March, and in desperation bought a Lotus 70 Formula 5000 'wedge' for Chris to drive in the Grand Prix at Pukekohe. After two pit stops Chris finished ninth. In practice at Wigram the Chevrolet V8 failed, and with no replacement Chris went back to the March 701 and finished fifth. He drove a few of the Australian races and commuted to Argentina between events to win the Grand Prix there for Matra. It was not a Tasman Series he wanted to remember.

10 French connection: Matra the might have been

In his two seasons with the French Matra team in 1971–72 Chris flirted with success. He was also one of the best-paid drivers, earning £1000 a week, which pales into insignificance next to Michael Schumacher's Ferrari income in the new century, but in those days it was a recognition of Chris's rating as the near equal of Stewart and Rindt. He really was that good. In addition to his natural style, he was a top test driver. The Matra MS120B V12 was a development of the 1970 car rated by *Autosport* Formula One editor Nigel Roebuck as 'the best-handling chassis in the business, but a V12 engine lamentably short of horsepower'. When Chris was preparing for his first season with the French team, he told Roebuck: 'I'm really going to try and get back to where I was in 1968 with Ferrari. Go for runs, cut down on the booze and keep the cigarettes under some sort of control.' When he last saw Christopher 30 years later, Roebuck observed that 'He was still working at it.'

As his luck would have it, Chris won his first Formula One race for Matra at the start of the 1971 season, in Argentina — but the Argentine Grand Prix that year was a nonchampionship event. It was run as a curtain-raiser to prove to the international governing body, the FIA, that the Argentinian organisers could host a world-championship event. The race was actually the second part of the Temporada Series, and was held a fortnight after the 1000-kilometre endurance race marred by the fatal accident that resulted in the death of Ferrari driver Ignazio Giunti in a crash involving Matra driver Jean-Pierre Beltoise, so Matra had only the one entry. There were no Ferraris, and the Formula One field was topped up with a handful of Formula 5000 cars. There were Lotus 72s for Emerson Fittipaldi and Reine Wisell, an older Lotus 49 for Emerson's younger brother, Wilson, a Surtees for Rolf Stommelen, and Marches for Derek Bell, Jo Siffert and Henri Pescarolo. Local driver Carlos Reutemann was making his Formula One debut in a McLaren.

There were to be two heats of 50 laps of the 3.4-kilometre circuit, and Chris was on pole for his first race with the French team, but he was bemoaning a misfire and a lack of torque. Stommelen made the most of the rolling start and Chris was swallowed in the jostling field, only just managing to salvage fourth place. Between heats the Matra mechanics changed a half shaft that had been binding on the splines. Battle was joined again in the second heat, and following a major out-shuffling between Stommelen and Siffert, Chris emerged in a clear lead and held it to the finish, drawing out enough of a time cushion to win the two-part event overall and set the fastest lap.

It was his only Formula One Grand Prix victory, and even that was not executed cleanly, being the result of a two-heat event of which he won only the second part. Mario Andretti was once quoted as saying that if Chris Amon quit racing and took up undertaking, people would stop dying . . .

Chris started in the centre of the front row in the opening world-championship Grand Prix at Kyalami and finished fifth, Mario Andretti winning for Ferrari. The decision to quit Ferrari would keep coming back to haunt him. At Montjuich Park for the Spanish Grand Prix, Chris started on the outside of the front row — beside two Ferraris. He finished third, behind Stewart in the Tyrrell and Ickx's Ferrari. At Monaco he was in the second row but his engine refused to start and the Matra was pushed from the grid. By the time the V12 was persuaded to fire, the leaders had done half a lap. A puncture pitted him, and just after half distance he was in the pits for good with a broken differential.

Chris was on the second row at Zandvoort, and in the rain he challenged Stewart for the lead going into the Tarzan Hairpin at the end of the long straight past the pits, but the Matra went straight on into the sand and the catch-fencing. He extracted the car but a radiator had been damaged and he was out of the race. Lack of engine development showed during the season when he qualified back in the fourth row of the grid for the team's 'home' Grand Prix at Paul Ricard. His Matra team-mate, Jean-Pierre Beltoise, was only 0.02 of a second faster. Chris finished fifth and Beltoise seventh.

Pedro Rodriguez had been killed in a German sports-car race the weekend between the French and British Grands Prix. Chris had known the Mexican well from Rodriguez's time in the Tasman Series with BRM, when he had been taught to play a form of cricket on the lawn of Chris's parents' beach house at Paraparaumu.

There was another fourth-row grid position at Silverstone, where a V12 with power should have faired better, indicating that the team needed to do further work. Chris went out with engine failure halfway through. At the Nürburgring the situation was even worse: he was back in the eighth row, and retired after an accident just after half distance.

The team decided to give the Austrian Grand Prix a miss and try to sort out their problems with the engine. 'It worked, too,' says Chris. 'Everyone thought we had a new engine but it wasn't that at all — they'd simply solved the oil churning problem.' There must have been a measure of Ferrari *déjà vu*. 'My engine at the Nürburgring only had 395 bhp while for Monza I had 460 bhp, which was now more or less competitive.'

Chris proved his point eloquently in practice at Monza. As always, elements of the French press had written that Amon was not the man for the job as proved by his lowly qualifying places. He had been through the same at Ferrari with the Italian press. He set blistering laps all through the Saturday afternoon session and was comfortably on pole with the blue

Matra, but in a piece of patriotic sleight of hand aimed at boosting the gate with the *tifosi* — the Italian racing fans — on race day, Ickx was proclaimed on pole with the Ferrari. It was only after the newspapers had gone to press that a faster time was 'found' for the Matra and Chris was given his rightful pole position.

Not that it helped, because Clay Regazzoni took a flyer from the fourth row in his Ferrari and led the field from the start. Chris and Ickx were swallowed up in the pack, finishing the opening lap in sixth and eighth places respectively. Chris had the additional worry of a left front tyre blistering, but he spent several laps getting used to the handling and then, with 36 of 55 laps gone, he leapfrogged the Matra from fourth place into the lead and stayed there for the next four laps. Despite challenges from Peterson's March 711, Hailwood's Surtees and Cevert's Tyrrell, he had the race under control. Then the Amon bad luck struck. Denis Jenkinson, sitting high up in the press section of the start-line grandstand, wrote in *Motor Sport*:

> With lap 50 approaching and only five to go the leading group began to flex their muscles for the final punch-up, and in readiness Amon took off his top face-visor which was dirty and oily, in order to see more clearly through the clean one underneath. Unfortunately both came off and he was left with no face protection at all, and that was all hope of a last minute battle gone for he had to slow down.

Chris finished a dismal sixth in yet another of the races that he *should* have won. 'Suddenly I got a 200 mph blast of wind in my face and that was it.'

At Mosport, for the Canadian Grand Prix, Chris started in the second row, and in a rain-shortened race struggled home 10th, three laps off the pace. Come Watkins Glen and the US Grand Prix, he was in the third row but picked up a puncture and trailed in 12th, two laps down.

The 1972 season started as 1971 had ended — badly. In Argentina, where he had won a year earlier, he qualified down in the sixth row having suffered a gearbox problem. In the warm-up the 'repaired' gearbox would only offer three workable gears and the Matra was withdrawn. In South Africa, despite starting in the fifth row he was up to third in the closing laps, but a vibration cost him two pit stops and he finished a lowly 15th, three laps down. At Jarama, for the Spanish Grand Prix, he started in the third row but retired with further gearbox problems. At Monaco he was in the third row again but the race started in teeming rain and he lost ground with four pit stops to try and cure a misting visor. He still finished sixth, but three laps down. At Spa, the fast open circuit he liked, he could do no better than a fifth-row start, and with eight laps left the Matra fuel pumps started to chatter and he dived in for more fuel, losing three places and finishing sixth.

Apparently needing something else to worry about, Chris had started his Amon Engines company. In early February 1972, *Motoring News* reported:

On Monday this week the first engine to carry Chris Amon's name was run up on the test bed at Vandervell Products' Maidenhead engine-test division. It was the new 2-litre Ford BDA-based unit which has been designed for Chris' newly-formed company by ex-Eagle, ex-BRM engineer Aubrey Woods and which will be sold for Formula 2 and 2-litre sports cars.

For the time being at least, the engine uses certain bought-out components, but Woods makes it clear that this is only a temporary state of affairs and that the all-Amon engines will soon be in production. An engine test-house should be ready by the end of the month at the newly-acquired Amon factory in Reading where Chris himself is presently overseeing the installation of his new company.

Two engines will be offered, a 1911cc and a 1994cc as a development with a bigger bore. Conversion kits will be made available to early customers who decide to use the smaller of the two. The initial trials this week should soon lead to full-bore test runs, and if these prove satisfactory the Amon-Ford will be sent to South Africa for further tests in co-operation with March Engineering.

Chris said he had 'quite a lot of confidence in Aubrey', and there were suggestions that if the Formula Two project was a success, they would surely progress to Formula One. 'Over the last three years I've never had a competitive Formula One engine; first it was Ferrari, and then with March at the end of 1970 the fast Cosworths never seemed to come our way.'

Amon Engines failed and was absorbed by the March Group in an arrangement whereby Chris would drive for March again in 1973 — or not.

'The engine company was supposed to be a commercial venture,' Chris says now. 'It didn't turn out that way. The engines weren't competitive, reliable or commercial. Aubrey Woods was in charge of the project, and we also did fabrication work for other teams. We made con rods for Matra and things like that. But it just didn't work out.'

Chris rates the 1972 French Grand Prix, on the Clermont Ferrand circuit, in the Auvergne, as one of the best races of his career. Jenkinson sets the scene in *Motor Sport*:

I was beginning to think I would never see any real Grand Prix racing any more, but the Grand Prix of France has restored my faith. By any standards, racing on the Circuit of Charade is what Grand

Prix racing should be, a superb test of driving skill with the best machinery that makes ordinary mortals like you and me mop our brow and mutter 'Cor!' The aces were *averaging* 100mph round the 5-mile circuit with its 50 corners, including two first-gear hairpins, and yet there is only one brief straight in which I could just see an *indicated* 100mph for about a tenth of a second, in the E-Type Jaguar. This circuit was not designed on a drawing board, it grew from the normal roads around the hills, which tend to follow contours of the land and take natural paths around obstacles like rock outcrops.

Chris had a new car for Matra's 'home' Grand Prix and he put it proudly in pole position, with fellow-countryman Denis Hulme beside him in his McLaren. As Chris recalls:

All season we'd been having horrendous engine problems — basically blowing up an engine a day for four or five races in a row. They were running titanium con rods that weren't properly heat-treated or something, and by the time we got to Clermont for the French Grand Prix we had literally run out of engines. In fact I was using a sports-car engine at Clermont. There was a difference in cams. The sports-car engine ran a three-ring piston and the Formula One engine ran a two-ring piston, so although there was something like 30–40 bhp difference on the test bench, the fact that there was less blow-by past the pistons meant there was less pressurisation in the crankcase, so in the Formula One car the sports-car engine probably had more power than the Formula One engine. It was actually the spare engine for the Matra endurance car that Beltoise and I had raced at Le Mans the month before. At the end of practice at Le Mans, Beltoise came in complaining of an engine vibration and asked them to change it, but they just revved it up and buggered around with it and didn't change it — and on the first lap at Le Mans it blew up. So I had the spare Le Mans engine for the Grand Prix.

Chris led, from Hulme and from Stewart in the Tyrrell. Stewart made it through to second place but Chris had a handsome lead. Stones started to stray on to the track from along the side, and several cars picked up punctures. Jenkinson picks up the story:

At 20 laps Stewart appeared in the lead, and the 50,000 Frenchmen around the hills groaned as Amon was seen heading for the pits with his left front tyre flat. With a ring of nuts to undo before the wheel could be changed, it was 50sec before Amon could rejoin the race and not only Stewart but Hulme, Ickx, Fittipaldi, Peterson, Cevert, Hailwood and Schenken went by while the stricken Matra was at the pits. In a slightly [EY: *slightly?*] angry mood Amon screamed back into the race in ninth place, making the Matra V12 engine give all it had got, and it sounded wonderful . . . Amon was really wound up and the Matra was responding beautifully, revving to its absolute limit, and twice more he set new lap records. He was gaining rapidly on Peterson, who had been passed by Cevert, the combination of one sick driver in a healthy car equalling out with a healthy driver in a sick car. Behind them was a very healthy driver in a very healthy car, and the Matra was right behind Peterson's March as they started lap 35. In one lap, Amon disposed of Peterson and Cevert, passing them as if they were not there, and on a circuit that is noted for its lack of passing places It was fantastic and almost unbelievable. Not content with that he continued this terrific drive and lopped four seconds a lap off Fittipaldi's Lotus in second place to Stewart, but the race was one lap too short for the courageous New Zealander.

As Stewart cruised home to a well-judged and cautious victory there were some 'Well done' cries, but when Amon arrived, in third place just 4sec behind Fittipaldi and still going like the veritable hammers of hell, there was a thunderous roar of applause and the grandstands, and even the pits, vibrated with the enthusiastic appreciation of everyone for 'the drive of the year'. With only third place to his credit, after looking a certain winner, Amon stood higher in everyone's estimation than if he had won the race. As one French newspaper headline put it: 'Bravo Stewart, but thank you Mr. Amon'.

Chris recalls: 'They had a hell of a job getting the wheel off and I think I lost a minute-and-a-half. I threw caution to the winds after that and just went for it. I ended up third about half a minute behind Jackie in what I reckon was one of my better drives.'

It might have been one of his better drives but he had still finished only third, despite the spirit of his chase.

That French Grand Prix was the turning point for me. After I lost that one, I really felt that *whatever* I did, it wasn't going to work. There had been so many things over four or five years, and I've always thought that after the 1972 French Grand Prix I never really had my heart in it a hundred per cent. I always *knew* there was something going to go wrong. It's a helluva lot easier to keep doing something if you're winning. I mean, confidence builds confidence. Jackie has always criticised me a bit for making the wrong decisions at the wrong times in the wrong places, but you get a bit desperate after a while. A lot of people have said I'm unlucky and I was jinxed and stuff like that, but there are two ways of looking at that. Some of the 'lucky' ones aren't here, so I've always sort of balanced one against the other.

Those with a penchant for numerology should ponder the fact that when Bruce McLaren won his first Grand Prix, at Sebring in 1959, his Cooper was number 9. When Denny Hulme won his debut Grand Prix, at Monaco in 1967, his Brabham was number 9. And Chris Amon's Matra number at Clermont Ferrand in 1972? Number 9. Close, but no cigar.

The remainder of the season was mediocre for Chris and the Matra team: ninth row in the grid and fourth place in the British Grand Prix; fourth row on the old Nürburgring for the German Grand Prix, the Matra bottoming during the warm-up lap, damaging an ignition pick-up, and starting late after repairs to finish 15th, a lap of the long circuit down on the leaders; third row on the fast Österreichring, chasing Hailwood's Surtees-Ford home in fifth.

The Italian Grand Prix at Monza was dominated by the installation of two chicanes to break up the glorious groups of slipstreamers, and suddenly there were huge brake-wear problems for all the fast runners. For all that, Chris put the French V12 in the front row 0.04 of a second slower than Ickx's Ferrari on pole, and for much of the race he was with the leading group or at least within sight of it, but with half the race gone he was heading down the pit lane with smoke pouring from the right front wheel, where the brake pads had cooked and expired.

At Mosport Park, for the Canadian Grand Prix, Chris qualified in the fourth row but an exhaust pipe fractured and the Matra slowed to an eventual sixth-place finish, a lap down. The US Grand Prix, at Watkins Glen, was the final round of the season. It was also Chris's French finale, and turned into a French farce. It was run in rain and mist, and the Matra engine lost a cylinder. With insufficient time to change the engine, Chris elected to start from the back of the grid. He finished a disconsolate 15th.

When the Ferrari team had totally lost the plot in 1969, with labour problems back home in Italy and financial turmoil with the Fiat takeover in the wings, Chris had had a meeting with Enzo Ferrari to suggest that it would really be better to pack it in at half-season after the British Grand Prix at Silverstone. Pedro Rodriguez had run North America with a Ferrari V12 in NART blue-and-white livery.

The same situation had happened at Matra with Jean-Luc Lagardare. He ran the Matra aerospace company so he was the big boss, and he asked me if I really thought they should continue in Formula One. I told him that we really weren't getting the job done, so he said, 'Fine — we'll forget it then.' Looking back I suppose I talked myself out of a Grand Prix drive with Ferrari *and* with Matra, but at the time both were lost causes.

I must say, though, that I look back on my time with Matra with mixed feelings. They were nice people to work with, and the car was pretty competitive some of the time, but it seems to me that the whole deal could have worked out so much better than it did. One of the problems with a huge company is the length of time it takes to get things done. I think John Surtees found the same thing when he was driving for Honda. You ask for something to be changed and it seems that everybody has to get permission from someone above them before it eventually happens. In the meantime there have been four or five races. The MS120D, which I raced at Clermont Ferrand for the first time, should have appeared 12 months before that. It was very odd: sometimes the car was competitive, sometimes not, and the Matra engineers themselves could not explain this. It went beautifully in France, hated the bumps at Brands and the 'Ring, and in Austria we had what Jabby Crombac called our 'holiday engines'. At Monza it was quick again, but at Mosport and the Glen once more down on power. I would say that, at its best, it was as good as an average Cosworth. I still think it was a great pity that they withdrew from Grand Prix racing, not least because that glorious noise will be absent from the starting grids of the world.

Just as Enzo Ferrari had delivered his assessment of Chris at the end of his three seasons at Ferrari, so Louis Stanley at BRM took it upon himself to pontificate at the end of his time with Matra:

Chris Amon is a brilliant driver, but perhaps too nice to be a racing driver. I would have liked him in our team though. I feel that in a BRM he could be a world champion. There is no doubt about it. But like Dan Gurney, he seems to have an extraordinary knack of picking the wrong team at the wrong time. I think he made a mistake again. Chris perhaps lacks the will to win, the mean streak if you like, that great drivers like Pedro had. He had an aggressive temperament, which Regazzoni has, and Surtees had when he was a younger man.

11 | Tecno fiasco: worst to worser

It seems hard to fathom why Chris would be talking terms with March to race for them in 1973 after the chaos of financial problems in 1970. 'It was the most extraordinary state of affairs and I never did get to the bottom of it, but basically once again it was March being March. We did a deal and suddenly the money had disappeared, so I agreed to start the season but wrote them a letter before leaving for Christmas in New Zealand asking them to use their best endeavours to find some money.'

The next thing Chris heard was on the radio — that he had been fired. He says he never signed a contract because no money was involved. After two seasons on a reputed retainer of £1000 a week, he had agreed to race for March for no retainer at all. According to Chris at the time, his letter to Max Mosley asked for a cut of whatever sponsorship money was coming after the South African Grand Prix — not asking for *more* money, just asking for *some* money.

My understanding was that Max Mosley would negotiate sponsorship for the season and I would be paid my usual retainer. This was in October of 1972, after Matra had confirmed their withdrawal after the Grand Prix at Watkins Glen. Decisions dragged on and it wasn't until the beginning of December that I was told I could have the drive but with no retainer at all because STP and Goodyear sponsorship only totalled enough to field the car. I had already turned down an offer from another team so at this stage was more or less forced to accept Mosley's terms. No contract was signed, but just before I left for New Zealand on December 17th, I wrote to Mosley and asked for a slice of whatever sponsorship could be arranged during the season, but said that I would drive the first three races for nothing as per our agreement. There was to be the usual prize money split.

Mosley apparently received Chris's letter having just read that BRM boss Louis Stanley had been making favourable remarks about Chris's ability, and he figured that Chris was intending to use March for the opening three races and would then switch to BRM.

'It was just an enormous misunderstanding. If I wrote that letter again, I wouldn't word it the same way, but I also think if Mosley received the letter again he wouldn't jump to the same conclusions.'

The result was that the infamous Amon noose was still around Chris's neck and he found himself sacked from a team he had never joined. As yet a further thorn in his side, March Engineering picked up the failed Amon Engines company while they were negotiating with him to drive in the 1973 season. Mosley said: 'Chris's engine business had gone bankrupt so we made arrangements to purchase those assets that we needed to set up our own engine shop [for BMW engines] from the receiver, and this was convenient for us. We knew the facilities and we were the highest bidder on the open market. Meanwhile we were still trying to put this deal together with Chris.'

The March deal collapsed in the protracted fashion that the racing world had almost come to expect, although Chris always seemed to be totally surprised when one apparently copper-bottomed opportunity after another blazed with potential and then fizzled out, fading to nothing. He could only move on — into the next of what by now was becoming a succession of complicated team situations, this time with the Italian Tecno team, run by the Pederzani brothers, based in Bologna, and sponsored by

Italian drinks giant Martini & Rossi. Tecno had started with karts and then graduated through Formula Three and Formula Two to Formula One, building their own flat-12 engines.

Chris was offered a choice of two totally different types of Grand Prix car, one of which would become the official Martini-Tecno, which he would race as of the Spanish Grand Prix in 1973. The Martini & Rossi motor-racing sponsorship programme was managed by pit-lane legend David Yorke. The tall, distinguished Englishman had been a motor-racing fan in the 1930s, flown Hurricanes in the RAF and been motor racing in 1949 with Peter Whitehead, the British privateer who competed with one of the first customer Ferraris. His reputation earned him the position of team manager in the new Vanwall team in 1954, with whom he stayed until they withdrew in 1962. In 1966 he reappeared as manager of John Wyer's team of Gulf-sponsored GT40s and the later Porsche 917s. Martini sponsored a Wyer Porsche in 1971, and when Wyer withdrew, Martini signed up Yorke. This was how Yorke came to be in the management sphere of the chaos that soon surrounded the Tecno Formula One programme.

Testing was due to start at Modena early in March, with a Bologna-built car designed by New Zealander Allan McCall, who had been Jim Clark's mechanic at Lotus. A British-built car designed by Gordon Fowell and Alan Phillips of the Goral Consultancy and put together by John Thompson in Northampton was due for testing at the end of March. Complicated or what? Thompson had been commissioned by Ferrari to build their Formula One monocoque tub in 1973.

According to McCall, South African designer Gordon Murray had been offered the Tecno design job but had passed it on to him.

I was hired to go to Italy and show them how to design and build a monocoque. I was given £10,000, which was a helluva lot of money in those days. I was the first white boy in Italy to design a Formula

One car and everybody hated my guts. I got zero cooperation from everybody except Luciano Pederzani. It turned out that it was quicker to build the car than design it, so I hired Eddi Wyss and we built the car from scratch in 10 weeks. We used the Tui uprights from the car I had built in England and we hand-beat all the panels. Pederzani was a brilliant machinist. He was a multimillionaire but he would come in every evening and machine up all the parts that I wanted.

The English Goral car started three months before mine and was finished three months after we'd ended the project, and Martini became very embarrassed. Pederzani was pleased with the car and asked me to find a driver. I suggested Chris and phoned and asked if he wanted to drive. In fact I left and came back to England after the first test day. It was all too much for me. Too much aggro. I got paid my money and Chris drove my car to a championship point in the first race they did, at Nivelles. It was the only one they got.

Chris went into the project with his eyes wide open, impressed, as always, with what he first saw of the team. As he said at the time: 'It's going to be embarrassing if the two cars are as good as each other but I'll have to make a decision by mid-April so that we can concentrate on one car. You can't develop two different cars side by side.' Famous first words.

Chris discounted the tales of discord between Martini and Tecno, which had resulted in the odd situation of two different Formula One cars being built for the same team, one of which would be chosen over the other. It was a can of worms, but he was probably so used to treading a fine line that the situation was what he had come to accept as more or less normal. The team spent all season agonising over the two cars.

Chris, again, at the time: 'Martini are more interested in doing well than in which of the two cars we will use.' OK so far, then. Another question mark hovered over the flat-12 engine, but team owner Luciano Pederzani said it had been cured of its appetite for head gaskets and there was hope of an extra 20–25 bhp and a working total of around 470 bhp. 'On paper it has the poke, but it remains to be seen whether it still has it in the car,' said Chris, philosophically.

In other respects, Chris seemed content. 'Going down to the Tecno factory was very pleasant. It seemed rather like going home — very reminiscent of my early Ferrari days. I've always got on well with Italians and there seems to be the same sort of enthusiasm in Bologna as there used to be in Maranello. It's a small unit but everyone seems very fired up so I reckon the deal can work out well.'

The McCall car was to be ready first and Chris had had his seat fitting. The Fowell-Phillips was to be ready three weeks later. Chris was reflective in his column in *Competition Car*:

I won't necessarily pick the one which goes faster sooner, but the one with more potential. It's a pity the decision has to be made at all, really, since it means that there will be a brand-new formula 1 chassis redundant before it has ever raced, but there's no alternative. Our season is beginning late enough as it is without trying to develop two different cars at the same time.

Bruce McIntosh, a London-born racing mechanic who had spent a lot of time in Italy and could speak fluent Italian, was working for Frank Williams when he received a phone call from David Yorke with the offer of a job in Bologna with Tecno.

I flew down with David to meet Pederzani, and because he spoke no English and David didn't speak Italian I conducted my own interview. I remember at one point translating from Pederzani to

David that if I was no good, he'd get rid of me.

I arrived on a Sunday and went to the factory to see Allan McCall, but they said he had gone. Gone? He'd left, so I never saw him at all. The car was there and there were a couple of drawings in the cupboard and that was it.

Gordon Fowell, who was designing the Goral car, was a fantastic engineer and I liked him immensely. He was very gifted. He tried to simplify, to make things easy. He didn't have an engine and we had a very limited budget, so it wasn't easy. It was also when England was going over to metric and it was a real muddle when we got the project out to Italy. I built the chassis at John Thompson's workshops in Northampton and took the monocoque down to Italy on the roof of my Volkswagen. Customs asked what was in the box on the roof and I banged on it and said, 'Nothing' — and there was nothing in the box and I drove on with no paperwork at all for the racing car. In fact all I had was the tub and the wishbones and the pedals. The flat-12 Tecno engine had never been on a chassis and there were no attachments on the engine, so I had to make up some form of tubular structure to hold the engine and gearbox and back end. Gordon would fly over every now and then.

Chris takes up the story:

First tests at Misano were dogged by rain, but when the track was dry the McCall chassis felt good until an engine problem curtailed the runs. Allan McCall had dropped a bombshell when he left the project. This was a clash of personalities more than anything else, and a great pity because Allan was a first-rate car-builder. I think he found it difficult to see eye to eye with the Italian way of doing things. I can understand that because during my first few months at

Ferrari I found things very frustrating, but I got used to it. I came to the conclusion a long time ago that, whatever the nationality of the team for which I was driving — be it French, Italian or March — they have their own way of doing things, and one has to adapt to it.

This remark may raise an eyebrow or two among those accustomed to the sometimes less than passive Amon acceptance of the way things were.

'I don't think Allan was with Tecno long enough to get to that point and I was sorry he'd gone. It was a pity for the team, too, because this was the time we were supposed to be sorting the car out and he wasn't there.'

Problems with the McCall car's flat-12 Tecno engine during tests led to the entry for the Spanish Grand Prix being cancelled. At this point Enzo Ferrari contacted Chris and asked if he would come to Maranello and discuss driving a third car for him.

The Old Man was in good form and said he wanted some technical input on the car, which you read as being a lack of faith in the technical abilities of Ickx and Merzario, who were the contracted drivers. David Yorke had come to the Ferrari lunch with me because I was contracted to Martini and he told Enzo that he wouldn't release me. It was supposed to be a one-off drive, but I think David thought that if I got a foot back into Ferrari, they'd never see me again — which probably would have been true, I suppose.

The debut of the McCall-built Martini-Tecno PA123 T-006 was in the Belgian Grand Prix at Zolder, where Chris qualified 15th in the eighth row of the grid, having been hampered by engine problems. Ironically, he was beside Jean-Pierre Jarier in the works March. He battled through to sixth place, utterly exhausted, to claim Tecno's first world-championship point.

In fact the decision to go to Zolder was only made at the last minute, because there had been overheating in testing and this was traced to engine head gaskets. Then the car was late leaving Bologna and was held up in customs, so I only did five laps on the first practice day. In fact I was agreeably surprised at the way the car went on the second practice day, but then the engine blew half an hour before the end of the session.

In the race itself I started with about 200 litres of petrol, which is a hell of a lot more than the Cosworths. The car was already about 150 lbs overweight, and with a full fuel load it just wouldn't go at all. I was in traffic from the start and I just got blown off, pure and simple. It seemed like every time I came out of a corner onto the straight, somebody would go by.

Then I started to get baked in the cockpit and I lifted off and just coasted. The problem was that the radiator pipes came right through the cockpit, one on either side. I wanted to finish the race because I felt that was what the team needed, but I had to talk very hard to myself to keep going. By the end of the race I really felt desperate, and in fact did my 'cooling-off' lap at close to racing speed. I just wanted to get back to the pits and out of that car. I was back first. When I finally stopped, I didn't recognise anybody in the team. I was in a complete state of dehydration, to the point where I was cold, having sweated myself completely dry. I also had burns on my back and feet, so it was really a very unpleasant drive.

Next race up was the Monaco Grand Prix. No testing had been carried out since Zolder but the water pipes in the cockpit had been covered, the nose had been reshaped, the brake ducting had been improved and the rear wing had been moved back. There were more dramas during practice: the engine blew on the Friday, and on the Saturday a water-hose failed and all the water sprayed out. 'There was a great cloud of steam and the marshals rushed to the car and showered it with foam. I was still in the car when they did this and I was *furious* — but at least I suppose they were erring on the side of caution, which hadn't always been the case at Monte Carlo.'

Chris starting in the sixth row, 12th fastest beside Beltoise's BRM and, interestingly, behind fellow Kiwi Howden Ganley's BRM.

I had a new engine for the race and made a good start, having a pretty good go with Wilson Fittipaldi in the Brabham BT42. In fact I have to say that the track seemed incredibly crowded in the opening laps. In earlier seasons at Monaco I'd been further up the grid with better cars, ahead of all the queuing and barging. Halfway round the second lap I had to come to a complete stop at the entrance to the Station Hairpin, and Wilson went past me on the inside at about two miles an hour — on the pavement. Then I had a problem with the brakes. I arrived at the chicane, braked, and the thing just wouldn't slow down enough. There wasn't enough stopping power to lock the wheels and the car clobbered one side of the chicane, breaking a wheel. After that had been changed I went back into the race, but the brakes had virtually disappeared by this stage because the fluid had boiled away during the pit stop. The car also felt weird so I decided to retire. Later we discovered that the steering rack had been damaged by the impact.

Chris was running out of patience with the fact that the McCall-designed car wasn't being developed because McCall was no longer involved with the project and the Fowell design was taking far too long to complete. He had also been pushing for more development on the engine but Pederzani didn't want to concede that the problem of lack of pace lay with the engine.

On the Sunday night after the race in Monaco, David Yorke, Pederzani and I had a meeting, and I suggested that the team devote all its time to finishing the Fowell car and that we miss the Swedish Grand Prix to concentrate the team's effort at home. This would give us time to get the new car finished and also to build up a stock of engines. I also made it clear to Pederzani that if we didn't get more power we would finish up dead last on circuits like Ricard or Silverstone.

Bruce McIntosh remembers that meeting vividly, since he was interpreting between Chris and Yorke and Pederzani.

It was a hot day and the windows of Pederzani's office were open. Pederzani insisted that I had to interpret word for word, and in an argument Chris could get quite fiery, although he was normally quite a passive sort of chap. He was on one side of the desk and Pederzani and his brother and an Italian mechanic were on the other side. Chris was telling them that the engine had no power and it was bloody useless and I was translating. I'd say, 'Chris, Mr Pederzani now calls you the son of a whore.' And Chris would say, 'You're a bastard of the first degree.' It was going backwards and forwards and I was translating word for word. It was hilarious, thinking back. Then Chris picked up a huge marble ashtray and hurled it across the room. It ricocheted from wall to wall.

Unbeknown to us an Italian journalist was sitting in the bushes outside the open window, and it was all in *Autosprint* that week. It was the start of the end, really.

Chris recalled an earlier dinner at Pederzani's home.

David Yorke and I were having predinner drinks with Pederzani when they got into an argument over something, and Pederzani stood up, punched David on the chin and knocked him out Of course dinner never happened after that.

We had decided to miss Sweden, get on with engine development and concentrate on getting the Fowell car ready for the French Grand Prix at Ricard. But two days later the Martini people phoned David Yorke to say that Pederzani wanted to do the Swedish Grand Prix. There were all sorts of obscure reasons for the change, and then we discovered that the whole team was concentrated on getting the McCall car ready for Sweden and the Fowell car hadn't been touched. It was at this point that our relationship really started to deteriorate. Here we had Pederzani saying we were going to Sweden while Martini and I said we weren't.

Pederzani was claiming that he would be a national disgrace in Italian motor-racing circles if we didn't go to Sweden. It wasn't the most amicable atmosphere I've ever been in, but we did get some sort of programme organised. Gordon Fowell said that his car would be ready the following week, but Pederzani maintained it would take at least three weeks. At least they agreed to miss the race in Sweden and I went back the following week to test at Misano.

The Fowell car had a lying-down radiator with the nose shaped to duct air into it, and I was keen to find out if it worked. We had experienced overheating at Monaco and I wanted to take the McCall car to Misano as well, to compare engine-running temperatures. Then, for reasons best known to himself, Pederzani announced that he wouldn't let the old car out of the factory. This was getting farcical, so David Yorke and I decided to go to Turin to talk to Martini in another attempt to get the situation sorted out. On the Monday before the French Grand Prix, Martini phoned in England to say that the cars would be at Ricard on the Wednesday, allowing us a couple of days of testing before official practice.

This sounded promising, so we went down to Ricard to wait for the cars. We waited and waited. We phoned the factory two or three times a day: the cars were about to leave, the cars were not about to leave, etc. Finally, on the Wednesday evening, we were told that the team would definitely be there on Thursday evening in time for official practice on Friday. On the Friday morning Martini told us that the cars would *not be coming at all* because Pederzani had decided that he wanted more money from Martini. Obviously his preoccupation with becoming a national disgrace through missing races had ceased to worry him by this stage. So we headed for home.

McIntosh says he was aiming to have the Fowell car ready for the British Grand Prix at Silverstone.

The first time I started the car outside Tecno's workshop it sprung leaks from *everywhere*. Petrol, water and oil came out of that flat-12 in jets. We cured all the leaks but we never ran it in Italy and took it straight to England, where I ran it up and down on the Santa Pod drag strip. There was a problem with the oil tank, I remember, and we buggered about with it and Chris drove it at Silverstone, but it was a disaster, the whole thing.

Chris was appalled.

They brought the old car to Silverstone for the British Grand Prix and in practice we were dead last on the grid. It was the first time that had *ever* happened to me. I had done a best lap of 1 minute 20 seconds, and Ronnie Peterson was on pole in the Lotus at 1 minute 16.3 seconds. In fact my time was exactly the same as I did with the Ferrari V12 in practice for the *Daily Express* International Trophy race in 1969. The Tecno was just bog slow.

Pederzani, of course, put all the blame on me. He told me I wasn't trying. On race day I was past worrying about the car. If we'd been in the 1 minute 18 seconds bracket I would have been annoyed, but when you're doing 21s it's not worth getting upset about it.

After the race the team pushed off back to Italy, leaving the new car for me to test. I tried it at Silverstone the week after the Grand Prix and I was impressed. I'd never driven a car that felt so right so soon. The chassis didn't appear to have any vices at all, but we were still stuck with the bloody Tecno engine.

The Dutch Grand Prix at Zandvoort was next on the Formula One calendar.

After the Tecno's pitiful showing at Silverstone, I didn't expect it to be much better at Zandvoort, and it fully came up to my expectations. It was quite hopeless. We used the McCall car most of the time as the Goral car was still unsorted. The chassis had really felt good but the engine had given trouble, as usual, so we hadn't had time to sort it out. At Zandvoort, the McCall car was handling very nicely but the engine was pathetic.

It was raining when practice started and I finished up third fastest in the session — I really couldn't believe it. Actually I think the thing was so easy to drive in the wet because it had so little power, and our Firestones were definitely better in the wet. For the first time in my life I was hoping for more rain that weekend, but on Saturday it was dry and that was the end of my hopes.

Keepers of corner times reported that Chris was nearly as fast as pace-makers Stewart and Peterson, yet he was three seconds a lap slower. 'Frank Williams went through his gear-ratio charts and showed that I was 15 mph slower than his guys on the straight. If I'd thought Pederzani had a drawing board, I'd have told him to go back to it.'

Chris sat in the eighth row of the grid, 19th fastest.

Coming out of every corner, someone would go by on acceleration — and then the engine started to cut out. This was apparently caused by a blockage in a breather-pipe when the car was on full tanks. I had told the Tecno people about it after Silverstone but they had done nothing about it. At Zandvoort it just got worse and worse, so I eventually pulled in and retired.

The German Grand Prix on the old Nürburgring was just a week later but the Tecno team was a nonstarter, mainly because their driver refused to go. 'I didn't want to go because the car would have been absolutely bloody lethal. When the McCall car was on full tanks, the front suspension was right down on the stops. There was literally no suspension travel whatever, and that sort of thing tended to show up a bit on a place like the old Nürburgring.'

The Austrian Grand Prix was next up and Chris wasn't optimistic. 'We were told that there would be some work done on the engines before the Österreichring but a couple of days later we heard that nothing had been done   the whole Tecno factory was on holiday.'

The Austrian Grand Prix was yet another Tecno fiasco. Engine failures during practice curtailed laps and Chris's best time was 1 minute 40.39

∧
A new red helmet and a Lotus 25 BRM for Monaco, 1964.

∧
The Chris Amon/Bruce McLaren Shelby American race-winning Ford Mark II at the Mulsanne
hairpin, Le Mans 1966.

∧
Bruce McLaren, Henry Ford II, and Chris Amon on the victory rostrum after the 1966 Le Mans 24-hour race.

FORD

∧
In the Karussel during the 1967 German Grand Prix.

GRAND PRIX PHOTO

∧
Chris Amon (2) and the season's world champion wait for practice at Monza, 1967.

GRAND PRIX PHOTO

∧
From left: much lamented former Ferrari team manager Franco Lini, Chris, an unknown photographer and Mike Tee.

GRAND PRIX PHOTO

∧
Amon in the pits with engine troubles during practice for the 1968 British Grand Prix.

GRAND PRIX PHOTO

∧
Receiving final riding instructions on the grid for the 1968 French Grand Prix.

GRAND PRIX PHOTO

∧
Energy conservation '60s style. Under tow and towing at Monaco, 1969.

∧
Flat out in the March 701 at Jarama, 1970.

∧
With manager Richard Burton.

∧
Winning! The non-championship Argentine Grand Prix, 1971.

Keeping warm before
the 1972 French Grand
Prix.

∧
Waiting for a turn in the BMW 3.0 CSL touring car at the Nürburgring, 1973.

∧
The final hurrah — in the pretty little Ensign in the 1976 Swedish Grand Prix.

>
Life today — Chris,
Tish and Murray, down
on the farm.

seconds, putting him dead last, compared with Emerson Fittipaldi's 1 minute 34.9 seconds in the Lotus for pole. Bruce McIntosh again:

> I was in the paddock in Austria changing an engine, but the only engines we had were from the McCall Tecno, which was basically a tubular chassis and nothing fitted. I remember having the engine on its end changing all the bits over. I'd been working all night. There was oil everywhere and running down a drain in the paddock. Tim Parnell came over and said, 'Bloody hell, chap, you don't 'alf choose the right ones to work for, don't you?'

David Yorke and Chris discussed the situation and decided it was best to withdraw. Then, just when it seemed it couldn't get any worse, it did. They tested at Monza a few days before the Italian Grand Prix.

> I started off with the McCall car, did two laps and the crankshaft broke. Then I went out in the Goral car and on the second lap this terrible vibration started somewhere in the engine and it wouldn't run at all under 8500 rpm. It was really quite dreadful, missing and banging all over the place. It got worse and worse, so I stopped after four laps and gave it away. We retired ignominiously to the paddock to catcalls and whistles from the spectators. That would have done Pederzani's reputation, which he claimed was all-important to him in Italy, no good at all. In fact it was a situation that didn't do anyone any good — myself included.

Chris told Pederzani that he would drive the car again when it was competitive but felt that it was all over. Another failed project for Amon critics to point at and award him at least partial blame simply for being there.

Once again Chris was at a career crossroad. As he said himself: 'Whatever decision I come to now must be the right one. I've made too many bad ones in the past, gone to the wrong team at the wrong time. I'm determined that whatever I do next year is going to work properly.''

Now came an offer that should have been a lifeline but was no more than a stopgap for the end of the 1973 season. Ken Tyrrell telephoned David Yorke to see if Chris would be available, and it was arranged that he would drive a third car in the Canadian and US Grands Prix alongside Jackie Stewart and Francois Cevert. Chris didn't know then, and few others did either, that it was Stewart's intention to retire at the end of the season. If it had been more widely known, Chris's inclusion in the team would have been taken as an indication that he was on trial for the 1974 season. But with the Amon way of things that would have been too perfect.

> The first thing that struck me when I drove the Tyrrell in Canada was the engine rather than the car. I did a few laps warming up and then started to put my foot down. After the Tecno engine the difference in feel was absolutely staggering. Suddenly I was getting a belt in the back again. You'd come out of a corner, put your boot in it and suddenly it was all happening. A V8 always gives more of a belt in the back than a 12 anyway, but comparing a V8 Cosworth with the flat-12 Tecno, the difference was simply incredible.

Chris's main problem was personal rust. He was out of form. 'I'd only done four Formula One races all season — and three of those hadn't been very long.' After the first practice session he was eighth fastest, slightly faster than Stewart, but it rained on the final practice and the Amon Tyrrell only made the sixth row, 11th fastest, beside old Ditton Road Flyer mate Mike Hailwood in a Surtees. Stewart was a row ahead on 1 minute 15.641

seconds. Chris's best was 1 minute 16.228 seconds.

I really didn't enjoy the Tyrrell in the wet at all. It was a development car with side radiators and quite a few major changes. When
the tail came out, it tended to want to come back the other way,
very sharply. I found myself thinking, 'My God, I wish I had the
Tecno here!' It was the only time I ever wanted to drive the bloody
thing. Twelves were much easier in the wet because they were so
much more smooth and progressive, and the Firestones on the
Tecno were undeniably superior in the wet. So there I was on a wet
race day with the car that everybody dreamed of driving . . . wishing
I had the car that nobody in their right senses would want to go
near.

At least Chris was consistently inconsistent.

The race started in rain and Chris drifted back until the rain stopped
and he could pit for a tyre change, but then Cevert and Scheckter crashed
and the pace car came out in a chaotic situation with nobody — least of
all the organisers — seemingly aware of who was actually leading. In the
midst of this Chris's engine stopped with a fuel-pressure problem. He
managed to restart but then a throttle rod broke, the engine went on to
full rich and he cruised like that for the last 20 laps.

Chris flew back to London after the race assuming he wouldn't have a
car for Watkins Glen because Cevert's had been written off, but the team
flew another monocoque over, the mechanics did three weeks' work in
seven days and he was back in business. As well as building a new car for
Cevert, the team had put Chris's car back to 'normal' configuration.

Still aware that he was short of track miles, Chris was working at his
times over the weekend, but just before the end of the Saturday-morning
session, Francois Cevert crashed his Tyrrell and was killed.

The corner where he crashed was very, very fast. I'd been taking it flat about three times out of five and Francois was going a good bit quicker than me so he must have been taking it flat every time. Once or twice I'd been pretty sideways there, and I think that is what happened to Francois. I think he just made a mistake, frankly, and got a bit too sideways. It was a very difficult corner and you had to be very precise.

I knew Francois well because we had both been in the Matra sports-car team and spent hours talking about flying. I've always loved flying, and Francois became fanatical about it. At Mosport, every night at dinner, we seemed to talk of nothing else. He had a great sense of humour but I think the most outstanding thing about him was his confidence. He had an incredible amount of it and always applied himself a hundred per cent to whatever he was doing.

The team withdrew sadly.

'So there it was. I'd been looking forward to those two races so much and they turned out to be two of the most miserable Grand Prix races I've ever been to. But I have to say that, despite my lack of success, I could see why the Tyrrell Organisation achieved such good results. The organisation and preparation were absolutely first class. Everything you'd expect.'

12 Amon and Amon: 'I just want to drive'

Like many men with more talent than confidence, Chris is obsessional in his pursuit of the best possible conditions in which to perform, convinced that he can only succeed with all the odds on his side. To this extent, Amon is less a competitive driver than a solo performer, capable on occasions of such virtuosity that most other performers who happen to be in the vicinity simply fade away.

Thus wrote Ted Simon in *The Chequered Year* with reference to Chris's first season with March, in 1970. The description continued to fit as Chris set out on yet another pursuit of the unattainable in 1974, with his own Amon Grand Prix car. 'More talent than confidence' — Chris's ability to self-deceive was little short of amazing.

'I want to keep my team as simple as possible and I don't want to get too wrapped up in the organising side of things. I just want to drive,' Chris wrote in his *Competition Car* column in January 1974.

So often in the past, when a driver has turned constructor, his driving has suffered because he's had to devote so much time to looking after his team. Bruce McLaren remained a competitive racing driver to the end of his life but I don't think he was *as* competitive as a driver of McLaren GP cars as when he drove for John Cooper. He was as much an engineer as a racing driver and after he started McLaren Racing, he had to devote more and more of his time to design and engineering. I'm nothing like the engineer that Bruce was, so I hope I'll just be able to concentrate on driving.

After years of tribulation and strife I figure that I owe it to myself to give myself every chance to put myself in a position where there can be no one else to blame

Dedicated Amon-watchers must have started to worry at this point that the man was exercising more confidence than talent, in contravention of Ted Simon's observation. The hole gets deeper: 'It seems to me that the best way of doing that is to provide myself with a sophisticated chassis, a Cosworth engine, and a small enthusiastic collection of people within the team.'

The Amon team was set up with finance from former racer and businessman John Dalton. Dalton had raced Aston Martins and Austin Healeys as an amateur in Britain. Designer Gordon Fowell worked at the team base in Reading. They would use a Ford-Cosworth DFV V8, and John Thompson would build the car in Northampton. Fowell and Thompson had both been involved with the second Tecno the year before.

'One of the great things about Gordon is that he hasn't been designing cars very long.' Only Chris could rate inexperience as an advantage in Formula One. He goes on: 'If that sounds like a contradiction in terms, what I mean is that he has no preconceived ideas and prejudices about formula 1 design and his ideas are fresh and original.'

Fowell was certainly a freethinker when it came to design. Before becoming involved with the Tecno, he had designed a quarry vehicle for an Australian mining company with tyres 20 feet in diameter and driven by a Bristol Proteus turbine engine, which drove a generator, which in turn drove electric motors in each wheel hub. He also pioneered Racetapes with his partner, journalist Allan Phillips, in the days before decent television coverage of motor sport. They made audiotapes of each Grand

Prix and mailed them to subscribers, who received them during the week following a race. After his brief involvement in Formula One, Fowell made himself millions with the design and production of running treadmills for gymnasiums around the world.

The Amon Formula One design pioneered the use of titanium torsion bars, and the team was the first to put the fuel cells between driver and engine, thereby placing the cockpit well forward. The torsion-bar suspension was fitted front and rear and there were inboard front brakes driven by constant-velocity jointed shafts. The light blue Amon had distinctive aerodynamic bodywork with the nose as an aerofoil section working in harmony with the wing mounted above it.

The three-day week imposed in Britain during the miners' strike in the early days of 1974 was not in the Amon plan, and completion of the new Formula One car was inevitably delayed, which meant missing its scheduled debut in Brazil. Australian journeyman racer Larry Perkins had joined the team as a mechanic, and Chris talked of building a Formula 5000 car for him later in the year.

Bruce McIntosh was also involved with the Amon Formula One project. As he explained:

That distinctive front wing and all the aerodynamics were done by Professor Tom Boyce, a Canadian who also did the shape of the Lola T70. He did a really clever biplane front nose wing, like two wings on the front combining the nose and the wing and the air duct for the radiator. It was all a bit radical and we didn't have the right set-up so we went to a straightforward system because we couldn't develop the original one. Time was always what we didn't have enough of. That and the finance to do things properly. The airbox was clever as well because we air-flowed the inside and nobody had done that before. Professor Blanco, a friend of Gordon's who lived in Birmingham, specialised in titanium, having initiated its use during the war.

Everything that was normally steel was titanium on the Amon. The Lotus 72 was the big thing at the time, with torsion-bar suspension and inboard brakes. It appealed to Gordon Fowell and he thought he could do better. I actually thought the Amon was a better car than the Lotus 72 but it simply didn't have the development or testing.

Surprisingly, McIntosh didn't rate Chris highly as a test driver.

We needed someone a bit more forgiving. Chris was a bloody good race driver, a magic driver, but I never rated him at testing. He didn't have the patience when he was doing his own projects.

The Amon was finished and run with inboard brakes that we had made up ourselves, uprights and everything. We had titanium springing with rising rate. The torsion bars were very short, about a foot long, and we twisted the titanium through 40 degrees. Gordon devised a rising-rate system whereby you bolted different plates on to adjust the spring rate. You didn't actually change the spring itself, you changed the rate of it. If we'd had more money, we'd have made different types of torsion bar. We never, ever had the time.

By March Chris was fretting at the delays and worrying that the complexi-ties of his new car would take too much time to sort out. The first race was to be the Race of Champions at Brands Hatch that month. They didn't make it. Initial tests were at Goodwood.

By coincidence, on 7 March the front page of British weekly *Motoring News* headlined two new Formula One cars by New Zealanders — Chris's Amon FA01 and John Nicholson's Lyncar. Nicholson would stay on in motor racing, establishing his successful Nicholson-McLaren Engines company.

Amon's latest Formula 1 venture, his own Grand Prix car, certainly looks different. The family relationship between it and the Goral Tecno — Fowell's design as well — is quite obvious, but with inboard front brakes and torsion bar suspension, the New Zealander's team has clearly opted for a chassis which should be a long-term competitive proposition. All the fuel load is carried behind the driver and ahead of the engine bay, accounting for the forward driving position, while considerable attention has been paid to aerodynamics as well.

Chris recalls:

We went to Goodwood for testing four times, and the last day there finished disastrously. I'd done three or four laps and was still troubled with vibration problems. I was taking things easily, not braking late at all and being very gentle with everything. Coming into Madgwick — the right-hander after the pits — at about 140 mph, I put the brakes on and the right front wheel collapsed and disappeared. I kept the brakes on as long as I could and I really thought that I might get round the corner on three wheels. I very nearly did get round — but not quite. Obviously the inside wheel does more than you think. When I realised that it wasn't going to get round, I put the brakes back on and the thing shot through a hedge and hit the bank. The impact didn't feel all that hard but I suppose it was still travelling pretty quickly. The ground was pretty soft and that helped to slow the car. The monocoque wasn't damaged at all.

It was found that a constant-velocity joint had failed because the joints were rocking in the hubs and having to take a bending as well as a twisting load. Bruce McIntosh again:

'Jochen Rindt had suffered a brake-shaft failure on the Lotus so inboard brakes were out and we decided to change back to outboard brakes. We also had a massive vibration problem on the front end, but it was sorting out the general problems before we could get into the handling problems. We really needed six months testing but we couldn't do that.'

Motoring News seemed oblivious of the Amon testing dramas and continued to wax lyrical about the new design.

The long awaited Amon Formula 1 car put in its first tentative shakedown laps last week at Goodwood and turned out to be rather more sophisticated than the pure standard British F1 kit car. 'Most people will think we've copied the Lotus 72,' remarked Chris at Goodwood, 'but the only similarities are the torsion bars and the inboard front brakes. But we feel the basic concept of the car is different, really a lot more like the new JPS-Lotus than the 72. If you opt for a relatively simple car you can build it pretty quickly, sort it out fairly easily and probably be successful more or less immediately. It may take some time to get our car fully competitive, but I'm sure it will be worth it in the long run.'

The Amon uses a Cosworth V8, of course, with fuel cells situated between the engine and the driver's seat and completely surrounded by a deformable structure which continues forward of the cockpit sides. Front suspension is by means of unequal length wishbones and torsion bars, with constant-velocity jointed shafts to the inboard front brakes. Inboard De Carbon shock absorbers are fitted at the front. At the rear, there are upper wishbones, lower parallel links and radius arms with the suspension mounted between a sandwich plate at the rear of the axle and a casting bolted to the engine and transmission.

In the sphere of aerodynamics, considerable attention has been given to increasing downthrust, the nose being designed as an aerofoil section and intended to work in harmony with the wing which is mounted above it. Chris hopes to make his race debut with the car at the Brands Hatch Race of Champions on March 17, after which it will be flown to Kyalami for the South African Grand Prix. A second machine is now nearing completion and a F5000 version will be produced at a later date.

The only harmony in the Amon Formula One project must have been between the nose and the front aerofoil, as the *Motoring News* reporter described. But even that would soon change.

The Brands Hatch debut having been cancelled, the first race was to be the International Trophy at Silverstone, but after 15 cautious laps on the first day of practice, the hubs had been stripped. The problem persisted, so the team had to start again from scratch.

'We ran separate little hubs inboard near the driver's feet,' says McIntosh.

It was a beautiful job — a hub and brake calliper all in one that Gordon had designed. It was a nice little unit, quite rigid and all part of the chassis. We decided to switch to outboard brakes to try and cure the vibration and we drew up some front uprights and machined them out of solid billets of aluminium, putting the callipers on the outside. It was something of a panic measure but we made it all up and had the outboard brakes fitted — and then the rear uprights failed.

The Amon finally made its debut in the Spanish Grand Prix. The dramatic nose shape and front wing had gone and stronger front wishbones had been fitted. Fortunes, however, did not improve. Chris was one of the slowest in practice and dropped out when a brake shaft broke on lap 23. With Chris, when things seemed as though they couldn't get any worse, they inevitably did.

The team went to Monaco, where Chris qualified in the 10th row of the grid with Jacky Ickx in the John Player Special, but withdrew after discovering a problem with a front wheel hub.

It must have been a wrist-slitting summer for Chris, who *knew* he had the talent but was having his self-confidence shredded as his Formula One car promised so much yet delivered so little. The new Amon missed the Grands Prix in Sweden, Holland, France and Britain, while the Tyrrell 007s, which, like the Amon, had made their debut in Spain, finished first and second in Sweden and first at Brands Hatch. Team Amon was just trying to get to a race to qualify, never mind win anything. Success was starting to look like just getting on the track.

When the team finally made it to the German Grand Prix at the Nürburgring in August, Chris was ill, and his place was taken by Australian mechanic and reserve driver Larry Perkins, who crashed in wet practice and failed to qualify as a starter. Tyrrell, meanwhile, notched up another second.

Five more weeks of desperate development followed, and Amon reappeared with AF01 at Monza but was still too slow to qualify. BRM also had huge problems in Italy, the British team for some reason fielding an all-French driver line-up. Beltoise qualified in mid-grid but Pescarolo and Migault only qualified their P201s in the back row. In a move that appeared to magnify its problems, BRM signed Chris Amon — who had finally abandoned his own project — to join Beltoise for the final two races of the season, in Canada and the USA. Chris was the slowest qualifier at Mosport, and *Motor Racing* reported that 'neither BRM figured at all prominently, and after visits to the pits to complain of bad handling neither driver was classified in the results although they were still running'.

The final race of the 1974 season saw Chris's fellow countryman Denny Hulme drive his last Grand Prix and the McLaren team clinch the driver's championship (with Emerson Fittipaldi) and the constructor's title. Chris must have been contemplating joining Denny in retirement but he took a whisker of satisfaction from qualifying 11th (a lone BRM entry since Beltoise had destroyed his P201 on his second practice lap) and eventually finished ninth, two laps behind the leader.

'Dire' didn't even begin to describe the Amon summer of '74.

13 Briefly BMW: great to win at last

For the 1973 season, during which his Formula One dealings with Tecno steadily deteriorated, Chris signed with BMW to drive in the European Touring Car Championship. The CSL coupés had 3.3-litre straight-6 360 bhp engines. Chris wrote in March:

> I have virtually no experience of this type of racing but I find the prospect intriguing. Saloons are pretty quick these days: I'm told the car will be capable of 180mph given enough space. Le Mans is one of the races I shall do for BMW and it will be interesting to see the race from the other side of the fence, as it were. In the past I've always driven a prototype in the 24-hour race and I reckon the BMW should be vastly more civilised! If it's anything like my road-going CSL Coupe, it should be fabulous. I love that car. When it comes to road cars, I guess my tastes would upset the purists. I'm all for air-conditioning and automatic gearboxes! The CSL is not an automatic, but it's the next best thing. The engine is so torquey that you drive the car very lazily if you feel that way inclined; at the same time it's quick enough to be fun if you feel in the mood for pressing on.

Amon luck struck the Group 2 BMW drive. The first race was the four-hour event at Monza, for which Hans Stuck did the first stint. A head gasket failed, retiring the car before Chris got the chance to drive. Later in the year Chris spoke at length about his BMW experience:

I was amazed at the difference in technique with the BMW compared to a single-seater. Stuck was up to three-quarters of a second faster than I was but I was rather expecting that and it didn't surprise me. What *did* amaze me about him was his ability to go out of the pits and start going flat out immediately. That was incredible. He didn't seem to need to warm up at all.

The BMW feels a lot heavier than a single-seater and yet it still rolls more. That sounds like a contradiction, but cornering in the BMW calls for a completely different approach With a Formula One car you brake late but you've got to get it all slowed down before you actually go into a corner. If you go into a corner very quickly, all that happens is that you get a bit sideways; with these cars you've got the great wide tyres but not a great deal of power with which to alter the attitude of the car. Compared with a Formula One car, you enter the corner later and take a wider arc round it.

The Barcelona round of the series was snowed off, and at the Nürburgring the BMW drivers had major handling problems.

The car felt terrible. I just couldn't believe it. It seemed remarkably reluctant even to go in a straight line, never mind round corners. I'm sure it was a tyre problem more than anything else; it felt as if the car were rolling from one edge of the tyre to the other. Very, very unstable. I really think Stuck did a remarkable job in the early stages, keeping up the way he did. In the end he went off the road before it was my turn to drive.

My biggest problem with the BMW is lack of knowledge of the car. In fact I never actually drove it in a race until Le Mans. An odd thing about the car is that it is not at all heavy to drive — certainly not as heavy as the average Formula One car, and this surprised me.

Matra always rented a chateau for Le Mans, and this year BMW did the same but went one better. They got this huge place, right out in the country, with every conceivable amenity, right down to a massage. Fabulous. In fact the BMW organisation at Le Mans was absolutely superb in every way and the cars were beautifully prepared. Everything team boss Jochen Neerpasch has been working towards seems to be coming to fruition. Stuck and I took practice very easily, scrubbing tyres, setting lights and whatnot.

I did the first stint — at last I got a chance to race the thing! — and I was running with Dieter Quester in the other team car, both of us treating the cars gently and stroking along. Then came drama. I shifted from second to third and there was no third. Tried fourth. No fourth. Second again. No second. So that was that. Fifth only. I came in and that was the beginning of a long stop. The gearbox had to come out and eventually, with the problems rectified, Stuck was on his way. We were way back now, but the car was running beautifully and I really enjoyed my stints. For the first time I really got to know the BMW and, also for the first time, I started to go quicker than my team-mate. In the middle of the night I handed over to Hans and went off to get some sleep.

What seemed like only a little while later, I was woken with a tap on my shoulder. There stood Stuck, so obviously something was wrong somewhere. It turned out that he'd bent the car while trying to avoid a Daytona Ferrari that had spun in front of him. He felt pretty bad about this as it was his second shunt in a row, but there was nothing he could have done to avoid it.

Driving a slower car at Le Mans is a bit scary, particularly at night. You can see lights behind you, but it's difficult to judge the speed of those lights. We were doing over 160 mph down the Mulsanne Straight, but the Ferraris and Matras were coming past a good bit quicker than that. It simply meant that you had to watch your mirrors all the time, which was very tiring. I think I prefer being in a faster car in this sort of race. It's funny how everybody says they hate Le Mans, myself included. I think I hate the thought of it more than the race itself; in fact I was quite enjoying it this year.

The best part of any Le Mans is the shower afterwards. I got back to the chateau and spent about an hour in it — some compensation after racing for 14 hours and all for nothing.

In the midst of the mayhem surrounding Chris's Formula One career with Tecno, the BMW races were like a breath of fresh air. He and Stuck won the Nürburgring six-hour race.

This was my first win since the Argentine Grand Prix in 1971, and very good it felt. With all the drama and strife surrounding my Formula One drives this season, it's very pleasant to do a race with BMW. We all get on very well, the team is superbly organised and the cars are competitive. At the 'Ring we were using a rear wing for the first time and it was extraordinarily effective. We were more than competitive with the Ford Capris, which had previously enjoyed the upper hand. Their acceleration is better than ours, but the new wing made our car very stable. Our BMW had been all over the place in the 1000-kilometre race in May, but now it felt completely different.

A lot of people have said that using wings isn't in the spirit of saloon-car racing. Maybe that's so, but you can't blame BMW. Jochen Neerpasch's job is to produce the best possible car within the rules to start with. Of one thing you may be sure: if the adoption of wings had been easily feasible on the Capris, Ford would have done it long ago. Anyway, it was a good race for us on BMW's 'home' track and I think Stuck drove magnificently, especially during the middle stint, by which time all our opposition had dropped out. This was really nerve-wracking. I just sat there for the last hour, praying that nothing would break.

It felt really great to win. The BMW organisation has come good now and the wing should be really effective in the Spa 24-hour race. If people are screaming about the spirit of saloon-car racing, I would say that I don't reckon the use of great wide tyres goes with saloon cars, either, but we all use those. I'd like to see the width limited. Mind you, I'd like to see that happen in Formula One as well. Racing would be much more spectacular. Formula One cars are so much easier to drive now than they were five or six years ago, largely because of the wings and the tyres. I'd like to see the end of both of them.

The Spa-Francorchamps circuit over public roads had always been one of Chris's favourite tracks, just as it had been one of Jim Clark's personal hates. The paradox here was that Clark won at Spa on a regular basis and Chris never did.

I like Spa — but under the right conditions. One of the problems with the place is that the weather is very unpredictable and the Ardennes area gets a great deal of rain. On a super-quick circuit like Spa that's the last thing you want, believe me. And I must admit that one of the things that was worrying me about the 24-hour touring-car race was the fact that I knew we were certain to get some rain during that time. And that was the way it turned out.

In fact it was raining when I got there but had virtually dried out by the time practice started. Stuck went out immediately and, as usual, did an incredibly quick lap almost at once. I finally went out during night practice. It started to rain again and it really was horrific. There's no other word for it. I'd never driven a saloon car at Spa before and going out at night in torrential rain was not the way to start. I did five or six very gentle laps and then came in. The following day it was dry, but we did very little practice because the mechanics had fitted a fresh engine and we didn't want to wear it out. Stuck's lap the day before had put us on pole anyway.

Race day was dry but threatening so we started on intermediate tyres. I did the opening stint and there was a battle royal at the front but there was no way I was going to get involved, so I sat back in fourth place, about 200 yards behind, and let them get on with it. By the time Hans and I had done our driver change we were in the lead. But it wouldn't last. A wheel bearing failed when I had taken over again and had a huge impact. Changing it took about 15 minutes, putting us about five laps behind, so we had to increase our pace. This wasn't a problem but then a valve-spring broke. After that I had a real go and did several laps the equal of Stuck's pole time. I was really switched on and thoroughly enjoying it, but then we had more valve-springs go, followed by the valves themselves, and we were out.

I must say it was probably the most frightening race I've ever taken part in. Groups 1 and 2 saloon cars just don't mix. The speed differential was far too great at a place like Spa. There were about 60 cars in the race and 120 drivers, a good number of them inexperienced and well out of their depth. I don't say this patronisingly — it was simply a frightening fact. It's very quick and very difficult. Some of the guys in Group 1 are going around together having their own private dices, completely oblivious to the Group 2 BMWs and Capris behind them travelling 60–70 mph faster. In the rain it was a nightmare. I wouldn't be at all keen to drive in that race again. If it was a straight six-hour thrash for Group 2, it would be tremendous, but at night, in the rain, with lots of slow cars around — no thank you.

The next BMW race was at Zandvoort, and once again Stuck and Chris started from pole. It must have been enormously refreshing for Chris to taste success away from the ongoing doom and gloom of his efforts in Formula One.

Hans started this time and had a hell of a dice with Jochen Mass in the Capri, which was a great deal more competitive in Holland than it had been in Belgium. I reckon our wings were less of an advantage than they had been at Spa, and Stuck locked up trying to get past Mass and put a couple of flats on the front tyres, so he stopped after 45 minutes to change tyres and refuel. This meant that I wasn't about to drive for two-and-a-half hours, so I relaxed. Hans was really flying and managed to make up for lost time, but it couldn't last, could it? He was missing and then finally appeared, slowly, with no gears. I got in and staggered away from the pits in fourth gear. I'd done about three laps when there was this terrible crunching and grinding noise and that was the end of fourth gear. This left only fifth and there was no point continuing like that, so the car was pushed away.

Amon's last BMW race was at Paul Ricard, in the South of France. Stuck qualified on pole and Chris did the start, not entirely to his satisfaction.

I made my usual terrible start, and Pescarolo in the Schnitzer BMW led away from Ickx in the Alpina BMW and Quester in our other works car. I managed to get by Jacky and Dieter and closed up on Pescarolo. We were going pretty quickly and drew right away from the rest. I knew that there was prize money for the leader at the end of every hour, so I passed Pescarolo after about 58 minutes. It wasn't chicken-feed either — it was about a thousand quid!

After the hour I let 'Pesca' by again and was happy to sit there until it was time to hand over to Stuck. During his stint he kept the car in the lead, and when he came in he said there were no problems at all. Off I went and everything was fine — until halfway round the lap, when I realised I couldn't get any gears apart from fifth. I came by at the end of the lap and held up five fingers to explain my problem to the pits but they indicated that I should carry on. We had quite a good lead and it was quite a while before we lost it to the other works car. It was quite remarkable how the engine behaved in these circumstances. Some of the corners on the Paul Ricard circuit are very slow, but the car would come out of them under 2000 rpm and smoothly pull away. There wasn't much power, obviously, but I think it's quite remarkable that a racing engine could be capable of such docile behaviour.

They struggled on and finished third while the other works car, driven by Quester and Hezemans, won, clinching the European Touring Car Championship. Chris had revelled in the series while his Formula One career had steadily unravelled.

14 Ensign swan song: the end of the road

Chris's 1975 season started with the Tasman Series again, this time for Jack McCormack's US-based team, which had bought the rights to build the Graham McRae Formula 5000 car, rebadged as a Talon. 'Good car, lousy engine' was Chris's summing-up of the series. The engine failed in practice at Levin, and he could do no better than ninth on the grid and suffered more engine problems in the race.

> We took the car to Manfeild to run in a new engine before the Grand Prix at Pukekohe, and I set a lap time that I don't think has ever been bettered. At Pukekohe I qualified in the front row beside Graham McRae, but it was raining by race time and the team only had four rain tyres — and they were three or four years old. They were so bad that I had to make a stop after a few laps and switch back to slicks.

The rain eased and the track dried for the closing laps, which meant Chris was now 'accidentally' on the right rubber, and he was rewarded with fastest lap.

'McRae and I set equal qualifying times at Wigram and the timekeepers said we did it on the same lap, so we tossed a coin for pole position.' The reader will be unsurprised to learn Chris lost the toss. He also lost a cylinder in the Chev as he left the start but was determined to offer battle to McRae, until forced to pit after 19 laps with a cracked cylinder head.

Chris bemoaned his lack of pace compared to McRae, who supposedly had a similar car. 'We shared a garage in Christchurch over the Wigram weekend, and when his mechanics had gone home one night we weighed both cars. His was *140 kilograms* lighter than mine — and I'd been complaining about lack of power.'

At Teretonga the weather mirrored that at Pukekohe, with rain showers throughout the race. McRae and Chris were in the front row again but McRae's car suffered a collapsed wheel-bearing on the warm-up lap and was withdrawn, leaving Chris to take a comfortable win in uncomfortable conditions.

When Chris agreed to drive for Mo Nunn's struggling Ensign team in the 1975 Austrian Grand Prix late that season, they were running an underfunded but well-designed car with elderly engines. Nunn had been christened Morris Nuffield because his father worked at the Morris factory at Cowley and had been an accomplished driver in the lower formulae, although he had never made it as far as Formula One. Incredibly, considering Chris's reputation as a top technical driver with a uniquely sympathetic feel, Nunn told Chris he didn't want any technical input.

He said he just wanted me to drive. He'd set the car up — I was just the driver. I said, 'Fine,' but during practice and qualifying I'd come in and suggest various minor changes. I'd asked him to alter the rear wing and he said, 'OK, we're doing that.' I did one lap and came in and asked if he'd actually made the change, because it didn't feel any different. He hadn't touched the wing. He was just fucking me around. I'd had the Firestone engineers try all that stuff on me years before. I actually had the ability to tell these things but some people just didn't believe it.

In 1975 Chris was on a Grand Prix grid among drivers who had still been at school or coming through the racing ranks when he had started with Ferrari eight years before. He offered longtime friend Nigel Roebuck a ride in his plane to the Austrian Grand Prix for his 'comeback' race in the Ensign. Roebuck accepted although he hated flying in small aircraft. 'That weekend was Chris's first with the team, and Nunn and his people found it a revolutionary experience,' he wrote in his book *Grand Prix Greats*. '"He's incredible," Mo said. "We move the wing by a notch — and he can tell. We're not used to that."' Something of a contrast to Chris's more forthright interpretation of Nunn's reaction.

Race day was awful. During the morning warm-up Mark Donohue crashed on the flat-out Hella-Lichtkurve, and by early afternoon was known to have no chance of survival. The race was run in Wagnerian conditions — rain, black skies and occasional lightning. Everyone was glad to have it over. Chris had qualified 24th and finished 12th, a lap adrift. Roebuck again:

'In the evening Amon's emotions were mixed. Upset about Donohue, he was nevertheless happy to be back in Formula 1 — and relieved to be in one piece. "Schnapps!" he commanded at the end of the meal. "For everyone!"

'"Is he always like this?" Nunn whispered. "I mean, we've never had a driver who even *smoked* before, let alone . . ."'

Chris's last appearance in the Ensign that season was at Monza, but he was plagued with a misfire and finished 12th again.

At the end of the season he was entered at Long Beach in Jack McCormack's Formula 5000. Several of the team were driving to dinner with Chris in the back seat of the Chevrolet when a young Mexican, who had been chased for 20 miles by police, ran a red light and T-boned them.

We rolled down the road three or four times. There were five of us in the car and everybody was screaming, but [as a racing driver] you get used to knowing where you are in extreme circumstances and I got the rest of them out of the wreck. A cop had arrived by now and wanted to know if I was any part of this. I said I'd just stepped in a puddle but the cop said it hadn't rained for six months. I was standing in a pool of my own blood. My foot had gone out the window while the car was rolling and I hadn't realised it. My right foot was crushed and it took months to come right. I sued the State of California, claiming I was the victim of an irresponsible police chase, and was awarded $25,000.

With a new MN176 Ensign promised for the start of the European season in 1976, Chris was keen to be back in action, convinced that his talent was still there and that the little Ensign team made up in car design what it lacked in funding.

The first race was the South African Grand Prix, at Kyalami. With an earlier N174 Ensign Chris qualified 18th and finished 14th, but had been holding eighth until a fuel problem seven laps from the end had cost him six places. At Long Beach he qualified 17th but a broken exhaust pipe prompted a pit stop to make sure there was no danger of fire and he finished eighth.

The next race was the Belgian Grand Prix, not on the majestic full-length Spa-Francorchamps circuit where Chris held the lap record, but on the featureless Zolder track. Nevertheless, he was starting to get the feel again after too many seasons away from full-time racing. He started the new Ensign in the fourth row of the grid alongside Jody Scheckter in the new six-wheeled P34 Elf-Tyrrell and chased him relentlessly until the Ensign shed a wheel and the car careered off course to land upside down against a bank.

Was it the old Amon ill luck returning? He clambered out of the wreck as quickly as he could. 'I was terrified it was going to catch fire,' he said afterwards. A smack on the head blurred his vision for the rest of the day and his right arm and hand were painful. He was bruised all over. 'I felt as though I'd been on the bottom of a rugby scrum.' But this wasn't the morose, fed-up Amon of the recent past, but a confident young driver again — he was still only 32 — looking forward to the challenge of the next race, eager for Mo Nunn and his little team to have the Ensign rebuilt for Monaco.

Self-confidence is vital for a racing driver. Skill alone doesn't do it, especially for a sensitive driver like Chris, who could easily allow himself to become disillusioned and had a lot to be disillusioned about, his bumpy career having been devoid of wins and notched up instead a plethora of cheated chances. Since Matra had withdrawn from Formula One and left him beached in 1973, he had thought seriously about retiring from racing altogether and going back to the family farm.

If I was being honest, I'd have to say that when Mo Nunn offered me the Ensign drive in 1975, I thought I'd do one more season and pack it in. I wanted to do the season to prove to myself that it was still there — so that I didn't go out on a down note. I wasn't too worried about what other people thought. It was something I wanted to prove to myself.

At Zolder there were Amon fans among the mechanics all the way down the pit wall as he shadowed the skirmish between Scheckter's Tyrrell and Hunt's McLaren M23, feinting in alongside under brakes from time to time.

I was able to outbrake Jody but I was doing it from too far back. I was losing on acceleration because we didn't have an airbox, so all I was doing under braking was making up the ground I'd lost on acceleration. I was probably getting a bit carried away with the spirit of the chase because I realised there had been a graunching sort of vibration for about 15 laps, and on occasions the car got a bit squirly but I put that down to oil on the corners. It must have been the loose rear wheel toe-steering the car. Suddenly I had this enormous oversteer that I never looked like being able to catch, the car was spinning and then it was upside down.

Motoring News reported that the Ensign was soon straightened out but the cause of the crash could not be established. It was clear that one wheel nut had come undone, possibly as a result of being cross-threaded. There were signs of inner chafing on all the wheels, so shortened axle pins were fitted with locking pins further up the shaft than before.

At Monaco Chris qualified midgrid in 12th position but was still bothered by a painful wrist and hand. 'My right hand was quite badly bruised and I'd had a few headaches after that thump in the catch-fencing. I may have torn some ligaments in a finger because it hurt like hell to pick anything up.' He finished 12th, four laps down, having driven virtually single-handed on the demanding street circuit.

Amazingly, in the Swedish Grand Prix, at Anderstorp, Chris made the running. He was in the front row of the grid alongside Jody Scheckter, who eventually won, until Mario Andretti, in the JPS-Lotus 77, put in a last-minute flyer and demoted him to third place, putting him in the second row with Patrick Depailler, Scheckter's team-mate.

In *Motor Racing Year*, John Blunsden wrote:

Amon was in there mixing it with the leaders as soon as the flag fell, and at one stage it looked as though he would find a route past Depailler's Tyrrell to run third on the road and second in the race, due to Andretti's penalty for jumping the start. Amon, though, contrives to take his regular doses of ill fortune just when things are looking best for him. It happened in Belgium when he was worrying Scheckter, and now it happened again when he seemed sure to displace Depailler. Entering the braking area before the long right-hander after the start/finish line at the beginning of lap 39, Amon's car suddenly gave a shudder and began weaving as one of his front wheels started to wobble. He stood on the brakes, but only seemed to have any stopping power at the back, which was of little help as the car veered off line. It went though the catch-fences as though they were cobwebs and charged straight into the barrier beyond. Miraculously, Amon was nothing worse than badly bruised and dazed, and he clambered out more than thankful to be in one piece; it appeared that a suspension mounting had broken away. For Chris it was probably the most horrifying of all his recent accidents because it was a long time (relatively) in building up, and those agonising seconds before the final impact had seemed an age as he contemplated the inevitability of serious injury, or perhaps even worse.

The team missed the next round, in France, while driver and car recovered, but bounced back for the British Grand Prix, at Brands Hatch. Chris qualified fifth, again in the same row as Depailler in the Tyrrell. He was lying seventh when a water leak caused the engine to overheat and he was out after only eight laps.

So to the daunting original Nürburgring, where he qualified down the grid, his enthusiasm sapped by the breakages and accidents, which had been no fault of his own. When Niki Lauda's Ferrari crashed in flames, the race was stopped and Chris Amon announced that he would not take the restart.

He arrived at the scene of Lauda's crash to find six or eight other cars had already stopped, so he climbed out of the Ensign and ran back down the road to warn drivers coming up behind. He had time for thought as the cars were forming up on the grid for the restart. He was appalled at the length of time it had taken for an ambulance to arrive, and at the fact that if other drivers hadn't stopped to rescue Lauda, it would have been all over for the Austrian Ferrari driver. The track facilities simply hadn't been equal to the accident. He dwelt on a delayed start he had made in an earlier German Grand Prix, when he could have had a similar accident and there would have been no cars coming through for perhaps 10 minutes. Also going through his mind was the knowledge that his mechanical record with the Ensign had not been exactly reassuring. He said to Nunn. 'Morris, I'm going home. I'm sorry, but it's just bloody ridiculous. It took five minutes for the ambulance to get there. It's not on.' And he walked back to the pit, out of the race and out of Formula One.

Jackie Stewart sat quietly on the pit rail with him, not so much trying to talk him into racing as offering alternatives. He could perhaps have started, taken it easy for a couple of laps and then parked, preserving his reputation. But Chris was not to be swayed, showing what I considered that weekend to be amazing strength of character. It took as much or more courage to stop than it would have taken to keep racing. I think Stewart admired his resolve, too. 'Chris had made his decision and stuck to it,' he said. 'I wouldn't condone it — but I certainly wouldn't condemn it either.' Two days later, Chris and Nunn agreed to terminate their contract.

Chris had started the 1976 season knowing it would be his last in Formula One, although he had wondered about a CanAm race or two.

The 1976 Ensign season was meant to be my enjoyment year and it started off like that. I was competitive without really trying too hard. But then the accidents started happening and at the Nürburgring the car wasn't working very well. I was really concerned. If it was falling to pieces on benign circuits, I had to wonder how it would cope with the Nürburgring. Mo and I weren't getting on very well, and after Niki's thing I remember thinking that I didn't really need to drive it round there. I wasn't in it for the long haul and I told them to forget it.

It was widely supposed that Chris was so shaken by Lauda's fiery accident that it triggered his decision to quit, but he insists that it was not quite like that. He had already decided that 1976 would be his last season in Formula One — the finish was simply brought forward.

Ironically, Teddy Mayer had approached Chris earlier in the weekend at the Nürburgring to sound him out about a drive with McLaren in 1977, partnering James Hunt, who was on his way to winning the world championship that summer.

There was a swan song Formula One entry on the edge of a CanAm deal with Austro-Canadian Walter Wolf, but following a crash in practice, Chris, in typical tragicomic fashion, failed to start in his last Grand Prix — the 1976 Canadian at Mosport Park. 'I was coming out of the pits on cold tyres at about 40 mph but someone had dumped a load of oil and I just lost the bloody thing. I was sideways across the road and Harald Ertl came skating backwards into me at about 100 mph. He hit me amidships and stuffed my left knee.' The race report put it a little more delicately, describing his injury as 'crushed knee ligaments'.

'I felt I'd had enough,' Chris says today.

I'd been racing for 13 years, and the travelling, the hotels, the aeroplanes, the airports — the whole thing starts to get to you after a while. It was probably more the way of life than the actual racing that prompted my final decision. It had inevitably reached the stage where it had become a job, and I'd got to the point where I didn't actually look forward to the next race. I must say, when I stopped I really felt I'd had enough and was quite happy to stop.

15

In Bulls with the cows: back home but not forgotten

These days Chris and his English-born wife, 'Tish' (not 'Trish', and never 'Patricia', as christened), share their time between the farmhouse they designed and built near Scott's Ferry when Chris retired from racing, close to the wild west-coast surf of Moana Roa Beach, and a second home at Kinloch, looking out over Lake Taupo. The Amon family has farmed in the coastal Manawatu area since Chris's great-great-grandfather emigrated from Scotland in the 1850s. There is even a local Mount Amon.

After Chris retired from racing, he and Tish took over the family farm and converted its 1000 acres from sheep, beef and cropping to dairying. Life became dominated by 600 cows demanding constant attention.

Tish's start to the day was triggered by the alarm at 3.45 a.m. 'I started about half past four. I drank gallons of coffee and then drove to the milking shed. There were three of us to milk the cows, and then I went home for breakfast. When we were calving we had two herds of about 300 each, so sometimes we didn't have time for brekkie.' The cows were milked twice a day. Tish loved the life: it was about as far from the glamour of being a Grand Prix driver's wife as you could imagine, but there was the satisfaction factor to consider.

Tish had pet names for most of the cows, having hand-reared many of them. The first-born calf in a recent season was christened Murray, and Chris watched his wife feeding it gently, almost maternally. 'It's not called Murray, Tish, it's called two hundred and fifty dollars,' her dispassionate husband said, leaning over the fence. They had a Rottweiler called Tess, a gentle name that belied her rumbling bark at strangers, and his and hers

Suzuki quad farm-bikes. Farming was full-on for the couple, but at the end of the day they would wind down in their bar with its feature poster of Chris and a CanAm Ferrari. A whisky and water or two plus the perpetual cigarette and the old days would soon come sliding back into focus.

Chris handled the feed side of the dairy farm. 'We had crops that supplied the feed, we made grass silage, and I ordered the basic minerals we needed for the proper dietary mix. It was a major operation with 600 mouths to feed.' He was not bound by his wife's milking routine, which was strictly her department. 'I got up any time between 4.30 a.m. and 7.30 a.m. It varied. My office was the dining-room table and lots of cardboard boxes. I've got a computer now but I'm new to it and it's not my strong point. I suppose my role was that of prime mover. Tish was very much hands-on.'

Mr and Mrs Amon made a good combination, following their different daily routines a million miles from their former life on the Grand Prix scene. 'I was happy being a farmer,' says Tish. 'Of course there were times when I *didn't* like being a farmer, but there are good times and bad times in everything, aren't there?' They have since sold the main part of the farm, giving themselves the chance to travel again, something being tied to such a large operation had denied them, but they have retained a more modest 300-acre holding at Marton, 30 kilometres from Bulls.

There was a period of mussel farming, following a visit to the Marlborough Sounds when the family fell in love with the sea. They had a bach at Kinloch, on the north side of Lake Taupo, but the routine of farm life meant time for relaxation there was limited, so they sold the bach, bought a section in the Sounds and rented a house. Explains Chris:

I started to get interested in mussel farming and ended up leasing a couple of farms and subsequently buying one. Why I ever needed more farming problems I don't know, but I soon got into the swing of it. You could seed and harvest all year round but I ended up with a sort of share-milking agreement with a seafood-processing company. I've still got one farm with six lines on it, each one a bit over 100 metres in length.

We had a lovely old boat down there, a 48-foot converted fishing boat built around 1916. We had a lot of fun in that but the problem with the Sounds was the logistics of getting there. Even though I had an aeroplane, we had a real hassle each time we wanted to go down. We had to load up the whole family and all our kit at home on the farm strip and fly down to Woodburn, which was the airport for Blenheim. I had an old Toyota van that we used to keep down there, so we'd have to unload the plane, load the van, and then we had a half-hour drive to Havelock, where we kept the boat. Then it was unload the van into the boat and an hour-and-a-half in the boat to the house. When you got there you had to unload the boat and lug everything up to the house. And you could almost guarantee that you'd walk through the door of the house and remember that you'd forgotten something.

The kids loved it when they were young because there was so much to see and do, and we kept the place until 1995. My father died that year and the kids were getting to the stage where their friends were going to Lake Taupo and Mount Maunganui, and socially the Sounds didn't have the same attraction, so we made the decision to sell and found another house in Kinloch. Within 20 minutes of the marina we can be on a quiet deserted beach out on the lake edge and there isn't a soul anywhere. That's what's so great about New Zealand. You can still do that.

The house at Scott's Ferry is on 60 acres used primarily for producing silage for the Marton farm. 'Basically now we can farm when we want to.

We've downsized the farming commitment dramatically, but I'll always keep an interest there because I love the space around me.'

Chris's dogs are almost part of the family.

I always had dogs when I was a boy. The first one was a cocker spaniel, and then there was a golden Labrador. For the first few years overseas I didn't have a dog but in 1971 I decided to get a basset hound of all things, and then a collie. At that time we were only 40 minutes from the middle of London but you'd still find hundreds of acres of woodland to walk them without seeing a soul. We brought the two of them back to New Zealand with us but the basset died not long after. The collie lived to 14 and died in 1985. Since then we always seem to have had Rottweilers. Dogs have always been an important part of my life and I've always religiously walked them every morning. It gets me out walking and also gets me thinking, because you can do a lot of thinking when you're walking.

As a little girl, Tish Wotherspoon had tagged along with her father to races in the north of England, watching the cars at tracks like Mallory Park and Oulton Park. 'But I wasn't involved in the motor-racing circus at all. It was just a thing I did with my dad.'

Chris and Tish met as two parties in a double blind date. As he remembers it:

It was at the end of the 1973 season and I'd done the last two Grands Prix for Tyrrell. Francois Cevert had been killed in practice for the Grand Prix at the Glen and Ken had withdrawn the cars. I'd just come back and was in a low mood when a friend of mine, David Hall, suggested Sunday lunch — and he would bring a couple of girls. That's how we met. Actually, Tish was with David. We had a wonderful roast-beef lunch at the George Hotel in Dorchester, then owned by Gerry Stonhill. Tish sat opposite me, and one thing led to another. I made arrangements to pick her up again the following week. She was staying in a flat in Ealing and I got hopelessly lost trying to find it. I arrived two hours late, and of course that was before mobile phones.

Says Tish 30 years later: 'I'd given up on him and gone to bed.'

Tish went to several of Chris's races and remembers the 1976 Belgian Grand Prix at Zolder as one of her favourites. 'Chris was in the Ensign and having a great race against the two Tyrrells.'

Chris takes up the tale again:

I was having a huge go with James Hunt until he blew up, and then I was the meat in a Tyrrell sandwich with Scheckter in front and Depailler behind. That was fine until a back wheel fell off and I was upside down, wrapped in the catch-fencing. When I got back from the hospital I couldn't find anybody. Tish was in a tent with a friend drinking bloody brandy. I thought *I* needed the brandy.

Did Tish worry about Chris when he was racing? 'You do, don't you? I think the cars were actually quite safe back then, and I knew that if he was worried about anything on the car, he'd stop. I think that was important. I preferred going to the races so that I could see what was happening.'

Tish remembers that Chris was not good at organisational detail in any aspect of his life.

He kept saying that he was going back to New Zealand, and I just kept quiet and wondered whether I was included in these plans. Eventually I asked him, and he said of course I was. I asked him if that meant marriage, or were we going to continue as we were? So he gave me some money and said I'd better go and buy an engagement ring, so I took it that that meant we were going to be married. I went to Reading to shop and when I asked to look at engagement rings, every jeweller looked straight at my tummy. Romance isn't dead, is it?

We were married in a register office in 1977. I was so pissed off that we couldn't be married in a church because Chris had been married before that I wore black. Black from head to foot.

Tish arrived in New Zealand to meet Chris's parents in April 1977. New Zealand in those days was at least a decade behind Britain in a whole manner of things, and while Tish was prepared for this, she found some aspects of Kiwi rural life verging on the prehistoric.

'I remember asking Chris's Mum about the black box on the wall. What was it? "That's a telephone, dear. Don't you have those in England?" It was like stepping back in time. We were on a party line with 10 other families. Can you imagine? It was like that until 1981, about the time the twins were born.'

Shortly after arriving in Bulls, Tish began to experience stomach pains and visited the local doctor, who asked whether there was any chance that she might be pregnant. Tish said emphatically not, but the doctor was right and Tish was wrong, and she then had to try to track Chris down in Canada, where he was racing, to tell him they were going to be parents. 'Imagine sharing a party line with 10 other households and trying to get a line to Sainte Jovite in Quebec to tell Chris news like that!' Amazingly, Chris had made the decision that very morning that his racing days were over, and this was the news Tish wanted to hear when she finally got through.

The Amons have a daughter, Georgina — 'gorgeous George' — and twin boys, Alex and James, in their twenties. Georgina was a veterinarian nurse in a major practice in nearby Feilding but has switched to midwifery. Alex is doing sports management and James is working in the field of human performance. Both young men are extremely competitive at sport. 'Being twins, they tended to compete all the time,' says their proud father. When they were babies they had to be fed in separate rooms because they threw food at each other. 'They had no problem tackling in rugby because they were always tackling each other on the lawn at home. They are both wingers and both really fast. When they play cricket, one is a really good bowler and the other is a top batsman, because that's the way they played against each other at home.'

Although Chris's children are aware of his reputation as a racing driver they are scarcely petrol-heads — but that could change. 'George went to Melbourne to see her first Grand Prix a few years back with my brother Bill, who has been a Formula One mechanic,' says Tish. 'She was absolutely hooked. Then the boys went to the British Grand Prix at Silverstone and just loved it. It was a whole new world. This is what their father used to do!'

Chris still watches the Formula One races on television.

In 2003 I went as a guest of Toyota to the Australian Grand Prix, at Albert Park in Melbourne. I hadn't been to a Grand Prix since 1976 and the sheer size of the infrastructure simply left me speechless. For people who go to races on a regular basis growth is an evolving thing, but to me the difference between my day and now was simply mind-boggling. I rapidly came to the conclusion that the only similarity to my time was that the main objective was still to be the first to see the chequered flag on Sunday afternoon. Apart from that there didn't seem to be anything that was even vaguely the same.

The cars are so high-tech now that it's a different world. I think I'd struggle just to get one out of the pit lane. In my day at Ferrari we had, including the engine shop, the gearbox department and the foundry, a racing department that probably amounted to about 100 people. And they were doing the whole car with all their own castings. Bear in mind, too, that as well as Formula One we did Formula Two, long-distance sports cars, CanAm sports cars and the Tasman cars. I believe that the Ferrari racing department today is over 500 people, and they only do 16 or 17 Formula One races a year.

A large proportion of the team today is made up of specialists in telemetry and aerodynamics. The impression I got talking with the Toyota engineers was that with modern technology they could pretty much run the car from the pit lane without a driver.

Hopefully this will all change with the rule changes to ban traction control and launch control. In my day you drove as much with the throttle as you did with the steering wheel in terms of steering the thing. If you've got traction control, you can't do that. I also have difficulty accepting the automatic gear-changing they've got now. Hopefully that will be banned as well and we'll get a bit more of the driver back into the equation.

Did I have any regrets about leaving racing? No. I was ready to stop. I joined very young and I got out comparatively early, I suppose. I was 32–33. Basically I'd been over in Europe from 1963 until 1976 and I was tired of the travelling, the nomadic existence. I wanted some roots. I missed my teenage years, really. I could have gone on for another six or seven years but I had no desire to, and once you lose the desire, you start to lose the edge too. I'd had enough.

A new career opening that allowed Chris to apply his talent as a test driver and gave him a break from the pressures of the farm came about almost accidentally.

In the early 1980s I worked on a New Zealand television motoring programme, road-testing new cars and commenting on them. I drove a number of Japanese cars, including Toyotas, and was fairly scathing about their steering, straight-line stability, handling and ride comfort. Having lived in Europe for 20 years driving European cars, it was easy to appreciate the quality of engineering in the Japanese cars, but it was fair to say that I was highly critical of their driving characteristics.

Some months after the last programme had screened, I got a phone call out of the blue from a chap at Toyota New Zealand who said he wanted to come and see me. I had no idea what it was about and he didn't want to talk about it on the telephone. When we met, he said they had noted my criticisms of their product and he suggested that I might like to put my money where my mouth was and see if I could help fix their problems for them.

I started with Toyota New Zealand in 1983 and the first car we did was a frontwheel-drive Corolla. Toyota had sent a trial-build preproduction car down from Japan, and I have to say I approached the project with a degree of trepidation because while testing and development had always been my forte and major interest in racing, I was obviously now looking for a different result. But once I got started I realised that all the basic components I was working with, such as springs, shock absorbers, anti-roll bars and tyres were very much what I'd been working with in racing, so in terms of achieving an improvement by testing I was doing pretty much what I'd been doing in Formula One.

One thing that had to be taken into consideration for a road car was ride comfort, but it became apparent early on in the programme that we could achieve a good handling balance as well as good ride comfort.

In the early stages we were changing the specifications but when we started to get prototypes sent from Japan with a team of Japanese development people, rather than change the specification we were able to create one.

I thought it was important to take the Japanese test teams on an extended drive of three or four hundred kilometres as soon as they arrived, to get them acclimatised to our roads and driving so that they could appreciate what we were trying to achieve, because driving in New Zealand is totally different from driving in Japan, with all their speed limits.

Ashton Rowe joined Toyota New Zealand a month or two before I did and he was very much a key link on our project. I was a development person in terms of feel and knowing what I wanted, but the calculation side of things was Ash's special area. We worked well as a team.

I've always cherished my relationship with Toyota, and it's interesting to see how things have progressed over the 20-odd years I've been involved. I've made several trips to Japan, testing a range of cars from the Corollas to the twin-turbo Supras. Toyota has two test tracks — Higashi at Fuji and the amazing facility at Shabetsu with various courses including an oval, which is seriously fun at high speed. I've done a 230 kph lap there in a standard 5-speed Camry.

I don't have any input on the Formula One side with Toyota. It would be pushing it to pretend I could be of any assistance now. Although they use similar components to those we used in my day, the way they use them now is totally different. At the 2003

Australian Grand Prix I found the cars were so much faster than they appear on television. And the noise! They gave me earplugs, which I didn't use during the opening laps because I wanted to listen, but I soon put them in because my ears were really hurting.

In the Toyota pit garage they had a huge working area for the cars, then a computer room, a tyre room, a parts room, a fully equipped restaurant, a place for the media to be entertained, and the drivers had their own massage and changing area. In my day we changed in the back of the team's transporter if we were lucky. At Watkins Glen for the US Grand Prix we had to change in the big garage building in full view of everybody walking through.

My time with Toyota has been a significant part of my life and many of the personnel and executives I started out with are still there today, so it's been very much an ongoing family atmosphere. When the farm was going through a fairly depressing time, getting away to test drive the Toyotas brought me back to the farm with a fresh mind. When I started working with them they were about number six in the marketplace in New Zealand, and while I'm not saying that it's because of my involvement, they've been number one now for years. I've been amazingly lucky to have the opportunity to enjoy three different careers in my lifetime and to end up with a combination of driving and farming.

Chris's two worlds were combined after a group of top Toyota management representatives from Japan attended the debut of the new Toyota Formula One car at the Australian Grand Prix in 2002 and visited the company's New Zealand operation during their trip. It was arranged for Chris to demonstrate his early Cooper on the Manfeild circuit, near Toyota's main offices in Palmerston North — David McKay's 'Old Nail', now owned and immaculately restored by Alan Drinkrow in Auckland.

McKay understood the Cooper to have been the 2.5-litre car Bruce McLaren drove to win the 1959 US Grand Prix at Sebring, but more recent research suggests it is actually the Cooper Jack Brabham drove during the same season when he won his first world championship.

'It was unfortunate that the car had been sitting on its old tyres in a museum for a long time and they had become flat-spotted at the bottom, which made anything close to 100 mph a really shuddering adventure.'

In the millennium year, TV producer John Milligan produced a television documentary called *Trio at the Top* (also the title of Des Mahoney's 1970 book on the same three drivers). The documentary was stunning. When it aired in New Zealand, the whole country was talking about it the next day, mostly in highly complimentary terms. Viewers who knew little and cared even less about motor racing were frankly amazed to learn that McLaren, Hulme and Amon were all New Zealanders. It was the old problem of having been heroes too soon. The three drivers made their names in motor sport before international television brought top events to living rooms in every corner of the world. Chris Amon — the bloke with the dairy farm at Bulls, the little furrow-browed guy with the thinning hair on the Toyota ads — led the Ferrari team 30 years ago just like Michael Schumacher? They found it hard to believe.

Milligan asked if I would deliver his questions when we set up an interview with Chris in the bar at his home. When I asked why, he said he thought Chris would deliver the answers better if I was doing the asking. I guess he may have been right. When I read the transcript again now, I can see Chris growing more relaxed, moving in to his answers, thinking about a reply that he probably wouldn't have thought about making in answer to a cold call. It was the real, authentic Amon, reliving the days when he led the best Grand Prix teams in Italy and, later, in France, the Kiwi who won the 24-hour race at Le Mans.

To my mind, Chris is an unlikely hero — mainly, I suppose, because I've always known him as a mate first and a racing driver second. As we have seen, Nigel Roebuck observed that Chris was someone he would have been proud to count as a friend even if he hadn't been a racing driver. But to the fans of the '60s, Chris was their Michael Schumacher. Three decades on journalist Chris Balfe wrote about meeting Chris in the Silverstone paddock in the days when a Grand Prix paddock was accessible.

I was that dumb-looking kid, the gangly fifteen-year-old with the blue jacket adorned with Ferrari, Shell, Firestone and New Zealand badges. My hero, Chris Amon, was driving in the British GP, and the following day (Sunday) was his birthday. I'd rehearsed it all. I'd politely ask him to sign my programme together with my '68 edition of 'Autocourse' — then wish him a very happy birthday for the following day. What could possibly go wrong?

It was a nightmare. There he was, parked behind the Ferrari pit in a Fiat 124. Next to him sat another hero, Pedro Rodriguez. I leaned into the car, autograph book in one hand, and foolishly an ice-cream in the other. 'Happy birthday Chris,' I blurted out, as the ice-cream fell in his lap. Amon and Rodriguez burst into laughter and signed my books. I hastily thanked them and ran off, red-faced and mortified.

Farming on a remote coast in New Zealand is really about as far as you can possibly get from the glamour of Formula One racing, and Chris might be forgiven for thinking the world of motor racing had forgotten him. When he accepted Lord March's invitation to come to the Goodwood Festival of Speed in 1998, he was frankly dumbfounded at the army of fans that crowded around for his autograph whenever he came out of the BRDC. Very much not a forgotten man.

The Atlas F1 website runs a bulletin board devoted to favourite stories about various drivers, and at the time this book was being completed, at the end of 2002, the link to Chris Amon was a runaway with over 2000 threads, while a driver like Ascari lingered on around 20.

In 1993 Chris was made an MBE for his services to motor sport. (When Mike Hailwood was made an MBE, while leading the MV-Agusta motorcycle team, he told his puzzled Italian mechanics that the letters stood for 'Motor Bike Engineer'.)

Was Chris ever aware of being much younger than his fellow competitors when he first arrived in Europe? 'They did call me "young Chris Amon" for quite a while, and there must've been very few Formula One drivers who could say they had three-quarters of the grid from the British Grand Prix come to their 21st birthday party, as well as Colin Chapman, John Cooper and Ken Tyrrell.'

You could address a letter simply 'Chris Amon, New Zealand' and it would be delivered, but ask about Chris Amon the former Ferrari Grand Prix driver in the pub at Bulls and few will be able to tell you that he lives and farms nearby. That's fine with Chris.

The survivor.

Postscript

Nigel Roebuck

Today Ferrari and Michael Schumacher are hugely dominant in Formula One, but when Chris raced for Ferrari and led the team in the late 1960s it was one of the most underfinanced of all the major Formula One teams. Chris left in 1969, and in 1970 the Fiat money arrived. I suppose that was the story of his career. I remember him telling me that in 1969 his Ferrari programme included Formula One, a world-championship sports-car series, and CanAm in North America, and I'm pretty sure he was paid $25,000. He said, 'Oh yes, and we got free petrol vouchers from Shell,' as though that was a big deal.

From every point of view Chris left Ferrari at exactly the wrong time, but he was driven by the belief that he *had* to have a Ford-Cosworth DFV V8 to find out where he really stood in relation to Stewart and Rindt. I remember Rindt being interviewed at the beginning of 1970 and saying, 'I have only two rivals — Stewart and Amon.'

To this day when you talk to Mauro Forghieri about Chris, he gets emotional. Mauro was chief engineer at Ferrari when Chris was there, and he still says that, without question, Chris was *the* best test driver he ever worked with — they just never gave him a car worthy of his ability. It is Mauro's opinion that in terms of pure talent Chris was as good as Jim Clark, although I know Chris doesn't agree with that himself.

Jabby Crombac and I enjoy talking about the old days in the modern Formula One pressroom. Jabby is the longest-serving journalist in the game, having been in Formula One since before it *was* Formula One, and when I once mentioned Chris as the greatest waste of talent in Grand Prix racing, he said, 'Oh, *absolutely!*' and proceeded to rave on about him. He said in terms of talent Chris was absolutely top drawer. 'People are always talking about Stirling [Moss] never winning a world championship, but it's much more amazing that Chris never won a Grand Prix. It just doesn't make sense. With all that ability how could not everything, on at least *one* day, come right?'

Chris went ahead with the Amon Formula One project with John Dalton and the car was, well, terrible. The association with Dalton was turbulent, but I thought it was a sign of how much integrity Chris had that he gave his word and saw it through. Top teams were offering him drives, and 99.9 per cent of drivers would have phoned Dalton and told him that they were going to drive for another team. But he didn't. In 1974 they were trying to run the Amon Formula One car and it was terribly under-budgeted and also horribly unreliable. I know it frightened him a couple of times when front brake shafts broke and things like that. It started out with inboard front brakes, which were unusual at that time. Lotus made them work but they never worked on the Amon, so the team switched to outboard front brakes, which meant a redesign and cost more money.

I always thought that was the saddest time of Chris's career. To see him in this car with his own name on it, struggling to qualify — it really was a *shitbox*. He was terribly unhappy — anxious and worried — both financially and because the car wasn't particularly safe, let alone quick. Everything in his life seemed to be going wrong, and it would have been an easy way out just to accept one of the other drives he had been offered. It said a tremendous amount for his character that he resisted, because it broke his heart each time he did.

Chris had two close second-place finishes that were surely meant to be wins. In the British Grand Prix at Brands Hatch in 1968, it just *had* to be the day that Rob Walker's Lotus, driven by Jo Siffert, held together. It was a brand-new car that had only just been built in time for the race. The chances of it finishing were zilch, yet not only did it finish, it won. And Chris was right on its tail. The other time was in the Belgian Grand Prix at Spa in 1970, when Chris finished second behind Rodriguez in the BRM. Chris was convinced the BRM had a big engine. No question. He and Stewart and Rindt had outqualified Rodriguez quite easily. Chris always thought it was a bit of a scam because Rodriguez passed him going up the hill from Eau Rouge. 'And he didn't even have the courtesy to tow me — he just drove past me!' But again, how often did the BRM last, especially at a flat-out place like Spa? That day it just had to. Then there was Clermont and the puncture, Monza and the visor — and Barcelona, when Hill and Rindt crashed and Chris was leading Stewart by a *minute*!

Chris seldom comes back to Britain but a few years ago he was there for Goodwood and an event at Basildon. We were in a crummy motel and it was three o'clock in the morning, and he was talking about that awful seventh-of-the-month thing with Jimmy and Mike Spence, Jo Schlesser and Ludovico Scarfiotti. 'They always said that I was unlucky, but I suppose, at the end of the day, I'm luckier than a lot of them. I'm still here.'

Glossary of New Zealand locations

Ardmore is a rural area 10 kilometres (6.25 miles) east of Papakura, which in turn is 28 kilometres (18 miles) south of central Auckland city. An aerodrome was established at Ardmore during World War II. In 1954 the aerodrome hosted the first New Zealand International Grand Prix, and continued to do so until 1962, the year 18-year-old Chris Amon, driving a 250F Maserati, first competed in the race.

Auckland, situated at the top half of the North Island, is New Zealand's largest city. At the 2001 Census, the population of greater Auckland was recorded at just over 1 million people. Bruce McLaren was born and raised in Auckland.

Bay Park was the name of a purpose-built circuit that opened in the mid 1960s near Mount Maunganui in the Bay of Plenty. Bay Park was a relatively simple circuit comprising four straights of varying length, all connected by constant radius corners. Sadly, it had to make way for a housing development in the mid 1990s.

Bulls is the curiously named township that is located about 18 kilometres (11 miles) from the Amon family farm. Bulls is situated in the largely farming district of Manawatu, which is in the lower half of the North Island. State Highway 1, New Zealand's main arterial route, passes through Bulls.

Christchurch is the largest city in the South Island and is situated on the island's eastern coast. Widely regarded as one of the most 'English' cities outside of England, it has had a long association with motor sport and is home to both the Ruapuna circuit and the former Wigram track.

Dunedin is also located on the eastern coast of the South Island, and is 360 kilometres (225 miles) south of Christchurch. Dunedin hosted its famous 'road race' up until 1962, the year in which the 18-year-old Chris Amon climbed aboard a 250F Maserati and drove there for the first time. That same race saw Johnny Mansel, one of New Zealand's most popular and skilled drivers of the time, killed when his car lost control on Cemetery Hill. Contemporary cars never raced there again, though the track was later revived for classic racing.

Hunterville is the home of Bruce Wilson, Chris's long-time and most trusted mechanic. It was in Hunterville that the 250F was stripped right back and rebuilt by the Bruces Wilson and Harre. Hunterville is a small rural service town on State Highway 1, 35 kilometres (22 miles) north of Bulls.

Levin is situated on State Highway 1 — 93 kilometres (60 miles) north of Wellington and 56 kilometres (35 miles) south of Bulls. A tight, purpose-built, kidney-shaped circuit, 1.76 kilometres (1.1 miles) long, was built there in 1956. It closed in the mid 1970s, having been effectively superceded by Manfeild. It was on the Levin circuit that Chris had his first race in a Cooper in 1961.

Manfeild is a purpose-built circuit named for both the region and town in which it is situated. The region is Manawatu, and the town is Feilding, a small urban development 15 kilometres (9 miles) due east of Bulls. The original circuit comprised two long straights, a tight infield and off-cambered corners.

The **Marlborough Sounds** comprises the north-eastern portion of the South Island. It is here the Amons have their mussel farm and had a holiday house for some years.

Marton is a small rural service town in the Manawatu, about 12 kilometres (7.5 miles) north of Bulls. Huntley, the preparatory school Chris attended from the age of 8, is situated in Marton.

Mt Maunganui is located near the town of Tauranga, which is at the western end of the Bay of Plenty. The Mount, as it is known locally, is both the beach and a small mountain. A temporary square-shaped road course was laid out near the wharf.

Ohakea is around 3 kilometres (2 miles) south-east of Bulls on State Highway 1. Part of the RNZAF is based in Ohakea and the runways were used for motor races during the 1950s and early 1960s. It was at Ohakea that a young Chris Amon saw cars racing for the first time.

Palmerston North is effectively the 'capital' of the Manawatu and is 528 kilometres (330 miles) south of Auckland and 143 kilometres (89 miles) north of Wellington. Bulls is 30 kilometres (19 miles) to the north-west of Palmerston North.

Pukekohe is a semi-rural region 60 kilometres (37.5 miles) south of Auckland. When Ardmore became unavailable a circuit was built at Pukekohe around the perimeter of a horse racing track. This became the home of the New Zealand Grand Prix in 1963. The original circuit measured 3.52 kilometres (2.2 miles) but was shortened slightly in the late 1960s. Chris competed in the first Grand Prix on the new track in 1963 in a Scuderia Veloce Cooper-Climax. On the shortened circuit he won back to back New Zealand Grands Prix in 1968 and 1969 for Ferrari.

Renwick is situated in the Marlborough region at the north-eastern corner of the South Island. The temporary street circuit hosted 'round the houses' races in the early to mid 1960s.

Ruapuna is the only permanent circuit in Christchurch. Although Chris never raced there, the enthusiastic members of the Canterbury Car Club have not forgotten him and his contribution to motor sport. In addition to the Bruce McLaren Stand and the Denny Hulme Stand, Ruapuna boasts the 'Chris Amon Club' bar.

Teretonga is the world's southernmost circuit and is located near Invercargill, itself at the bottom of the South Island. It is often referred to as New Zealand's best track. It opened in 1957 and is still used for major meetings.

Wanganui is 44 kilometres (27.5 miles) north-west of Bulls on the west coast of the North Island. Wanganui Collegiate is one of the country's most respected and established schools. Although now 'co-ed', it has been a boys school throughout most of its existence. Chris Amon attended Wanganui Collegiate until the end of 1959. He took flying lessons at the Wanganui Airport while boarding at Collegiate.

Wellington is the nation's capital and is situated at the south-western tip of the North Island.

Wigram is a suburb of Christchurch and, like Ohakea, was a base for the RNZAF. The Lady Wigram Trophy race was first run at Wigram in 1949. Although there were slight alterations over the years, the basic configuration of the circuit remained until the track closed in the 1990s.

Chris Amon's Formula One Record

Races:	96	Debut:	26 May 1963
Wins:	0	Last Race:	3 October 1976
Podiums:	11	First Pole:	12 May 1968
Pole Positions:	5	Last Pole:	2 July 1972
Retirements:	56		
Points Accumulated:	83		

Date	Team	Car-Engine	Tyres
1963			
26 May	Reg Parnell (Racing)	1.5 Lola 4A-Climax V8	D
9 June	Reg Parnell (Racing)	1.5 Lola 4A-Climax V8	D
23 June	Reg Parnell (Racing)	1.5 Lola 4A-Climax V8	D
30 June	Reg Parnell (Racing)	1.5 Lola 4A-Climax V8	D
20 July	Reg Parnell (Racing)	1.5 Lola 4A-Climax V8	D
4 August	Reg Parnell (Racing)	1.5 Lola 4A-Climax V8	D
8 September	Reg Parnell (Racing)	1.5 Lola 4A-Climax V8	D
27 October	Reg Parnell (Racing)	1.5 Lotus 25-BRM V8	D
1964			
10 May	Reg Parnell (Racing)	1.5 Lotus 25-BRM V8	D
24 May	Reg Parnell (Racing)	1.5 Lotus 25-BRM V8	D
14 June	Reg Parnell (Racing)	1.5 Lotus 25-BRM V8	D
28 June	Reg Parnell (Racing)	1.5 Lotus 25-BRM V8	D
11 July	Reg Parnell (Racing)	1.5 Lotus 25-BRM V8	D
2 August	Reg Parnell (Racing)	1.5 Lotus 25-BRM V8	D
23 August	Reg Parnell (Racing)	1.5 Lotus 25-Climax V8	D
4 October	Reg Parnell (Racing)	1.5 Lotus 25-BRM V8	D
25 October	Reg Parnell (Racing)	1.5 Lotus 25-BRM V8	D

Fastest laps:	7 June 1970	Spa Francorchamps	
	4 June 1971	Nivelles	
	2 July 1972	Clermont Ferrand	

Circuit	Qualified	Finished	Race Report
Monte Carlo	DNS	Retired	DNS, car driven by Trintignant
Spa Francorchamps	15	Retired	Oil leak
Zandvoort	12	Retired	Water pump
Reims	15	7	Finished 2 laps down
Silverstone	14	7	Finished 2 laps down
Nürburgring	14	Retired	Accident, steering
Monza	DNS	Retired	DNS, practice accident
Mexico City	19	Retired	Gearbox
Monte Carlo	DNQ	Retired	DNQ
Zandvoort	13	5	Finished 1 lap down
Spa Francorchamps	11	Retired	Con rod
Rouen	14	10	Finished 4 laps down
Brands Hatch	11	Retired	Clutch
Nürburgring	9	11	Suspension; finished 3 laps down
Zeltweg	17	Retired	Engine
Watkins Glen	11	Retired	Starter motor bolt
Mexico City	12	Retired	Gearbox

Date	Team	Car-Engine	Tyres
1965			
27 June	Reg Parnell (Racing)	1.5 Lotus 25-BRM V8	D
10 July	Ian Raby Racing	1.5 Brabham BT3-BRM V8	D
1 August	Reg Parnell (Racing)	1.5 Lotus 25-BRM V8	D
1966			
3 July	Cooper Car Co.	3.0 Cooper T81-Maserati V12	D
4 September	Chris Amon	2.0 Brabham BT11-BRM V8	-
1967			
7 May	Scuderia Ferrari	3.0 Ferrari 312/67 V12	F
4 June	Scuderia Ferrari	3.0 Ferrari 312/67 V12	F
18 June	Scuderia Ferrari	3.0 Ferrari 312/67 V12	F
2 July	Scuderia Ferrari	3.0 Ferrari 312/67 V12	F
15 July	Scuderia Ferrari	3.0 Ferrari 312/67 V12	F
6 August	Scuderia Ferrari	3.0 Ferrari 312/67 V12	F
27 August	Scuderia Ferrari	3.0 Ferrari 312/67 V12	F
10 September	Scuderia Ferrari	3.0 Ferrari 312/67 V12	F
1 October	Scuderia Ferrari	3.0 Ferrari 312/67 V12	F
22 October	Scuderia Ferrari	3.0 Ferrari 312/67 V12	F
1968			
1 January	Scuderia Ferrari	3.0 Ferrari 312/67 V12	F
12 May	Scuderia Ferrari	3.0 Ferrari 312/67/68 V12	F
9 June	Scuderia Ferrari	3.0 Ferrari 312/67/68 V12	F
23 June	Scuderia Ferrari	3.0 Ferrari 312/68 V12	F
7 July	Scuderia Ferrari	3.0 Ferrari 312/68 V12	F
20 July	Scuderia Ferrari	3.0 Ferrari 312/68 V12	F
4 August	Scuderia Ferrari	3.0 Ferrari 312/68 V12	F
8 September	Scuderia Ferrari	3.0 Ferrari 312/68 V12	F
22 September	Scuderia Ferrari	3.0 Ferrari 312/68 V12	F

Circuit	Qualified	Finished	Race Report
Clermont Ferrand	8	Retired	Fuel feed
Silverstone	DNS	Retired	DNS, Raby drove car
Nürburgring	15	Retired	Ignition
Reims	7	8	Loose hub nut; finished 4 laps down
Monza	DNQ	Retired	DNQ
Monte Carlo	14	3	Finished 2 laps down
Zandvoort	9	4	
Spa Francorchamps	5	3	
Le Mans	7	Retired	Throttle cable
Silverstone	6	3	
Nürburgring	8	3	
Mosport Park	4	6	Finished 3 laps down
Monza	4	7	Pit stop, handling; finished 4 laps down
Watkins Glen	4	Retired	Engine
Mexico City	2	9	Fuel feed problem; finished 3 laps down
Kyalami	8	4	Pit stop, fuel; finished 2 laps down
Jarama	1	Retired	Fuel pump
Spa Francorchamps	1	Retired	Stone holed radiator
Zandvoort	1	6	Pit stop, tyres; finished 5 laps down
Rouen	5	10	Engine, tyres; finished 5 laps down
Brands Hatch	3	2	
Nürburgring	2	Retired	Accident, spun off
Monza	3	Retired	Spun on oil
St Jovite	2	Retired	Transmission

Date	Team	Car-Engine	Tyres
6 October	Scuderia Ferrari	3.0 Ferrari 312/68 V12	F
3 November	Scuderia Ferrari	3.0 Ferrari 312/68 V12	F

1969

1 March	Scuderia Ferrari	3.0 Ferrari 312/69 V12	F
4 May	Scuderia Ferrari	3.0 Ferrari 312/69 V12	F
18 May	Scuderia Ferrari	3.0 Ferrari 312/69 V12	F
21 June	Scuderia Ferrari	3.0 Ferrari 312/69 V12	F
6 July	Scuderia Ferrari	3.0 Ferrari 312/69 V12	F
19 July	Scuderia Ferrari	3.0 Ferrari 312/69 V12	F

1970

7 March	March Engineering	3.0 March 701-Cosworth V8	F
19 April	March Engineering	3.0 March 701-Cosworth V8	F
10 May	March Engineering	3.0 March 701-Cosworth V8	F
7 June	March Engineering	3.0 March 701-Cosworth V8	F
21 June	March Engineering	3.0 March 701-Cosworth V8	F
5 July	March Engineering	3.0 March 701-Cosworth V8	F
18 July	March Engineering	3.0 March 701-Cosworth V8	F
2 August	March Engineering	3.0 March 701-Cosworth V8	F
16 August	March Engineering	3.0 March 701-Cosworth V8	F
6 September	March Engineering	3.0 March 701-Cosworth V8	F
20 September	March Engineering	3.0 March 701-Cosworth V8	F
4 October	March Engineering	3.0 March 701-Cosworth V8	F
25 October	March Engineering	3.0 March 701-Cosworth V8	F

1971

6 March	Equipe Matra Sports	3.0 Matra-Simca MS120B V12	G
18 May	Equipe Matra Sports	3.0 Matra-Simca MS120B V12	G
23 May	Equipe Matra Sports	3.0 Matra-Simca MS120B V12	G
20 June	Equipe Matra Sports	3.0 Matra-Simca MS120B V12	G
4 July	Equipe Matra Sports	3.0 Matra-Simca MS120B V12	G
17 July	Equipe Matra Sports	3.0 Matra-Simca MS120B V12	G
1 August	Equipe Matra Sports	3.0 Matra-Simca MS120B V12	G

Circuit	Qualified	Finished	Race Report
Watkins Glen	4	Retired	Water pipe
Mexico City	2	Retired	Water pump drive, overheating
Kyalami	5	Retired	Engine
Montjuich Park	2	Retired	Engine while leading
Monte Carlo	2	Retired	Differential
Zandvoort	4	3	
Clermont Ferrand	6	Retired	Engine
Silverstone	5	Retired	Gearbox
Kyalami	2	Retired	Overheating
Jarama	6	Retired	Engine, clutch
Monte Carlo	2	Retired	Rear suspension bolt
Spa Francorchamps	3	2	
Zandvoort	4	Retired	Clutch
Clermont Ferrant	3	2	
Brands Hatch	17	5	Finished 1 lap down
Hockenheim	6	Retired	Engine
Österreichring	6	8	Finished 1 lap down
Monza	18	7	Finished 1 lap down
St Jovite	6	3	
Watkins Glen	5	5	Pit stop, tyres; finished 1 lap down
Mexico City	5	4	
Kyalami	2	5	Finished 1 lap down
Montjuich Park	3	3	
Monte Carlo	4	Retired	Crown wheel and pinion
Zandvoort	5	Retired	Spun off, damaged radiator
Paul Ricard	9	5	
Silverstone	9	Retired	Dropped valve
Nürburgring	16	Retired	Spun, damaged suspension

Date	Team	Car-Engine	Tyres
5 September	Equipe Matra Sports	3.0 Matra-Simca MS120B V12	G
19 September	Equipe Matra Sports	3.0 Matra-Simca MS120B V12	G
3 October	Equipe Matra Sports	3.0 Matra-Simca MS120B V12	G

1972

23 January	Equipe Matra	3.0 Matra-Simca MS120C V12	G
4 March	Equipe Matra	3.0 Matra-Simca MS120C V12	G
1 May	Equipe Matra	3.0 Matra-Simca MS120C V12	G
14 May	Equipe Matra	3.0 Matra-Simca MS120C V12	G
4 June	Equipe Matra	3.0 Matra-Simca MS120C V12	G
2 July	Equipe Matra	3.0 Matra-Simca MS120D V12	G
15 July	Equipe Matra	3.0 Matra-Simca MS120C V12	G
30 July	Equipe Matra	3.0 Matra-Simca MS120D V12	G
13 August	Equipe Matra	3.0 Matra-Simca MS120D V12	G
10 September	Equipe Matra	3.0 Matra-Simca MS120D V12	G
24 September	Equipe Matra	3.0 Matra-Simca MS120D V12	G
8 October	Equipe Matra	3.0 Matra-Simca MS120D V12	G

1973

20 May	Martini Racing Team	3.0 Tecno PA123 F12	F
3 June	Martini Racing Team	3.0 Tecno PA123 F12	F
14 July	Martini Racing Team	3.0 Tecno PA123 F12	F
29 July	Martini Racing Team	3.0 Tecno PA123 F12	F
19 August	Martini Racing Team	3.0 Tecno PA123 F12	F
23 September	Elf Team Tyrrell	3.0 Tyrell 005-Cosworth V8	G
7 October	Elf Team Tyrrell	3.0 Tyrell 005-Cosworth V8	G

1974

28 April	Chris Amon Racing	3.0 Amon AF101-Cosworth V8	F

Circuit	Qualified	Finished	Race Report
Monza	1	6	Lost visor while leading race
Mosport Park	5	10	Finished 3 laps down
Watkins Glen	8	12	Pit stop, tyres; finished two laps down
Buenos Aires	12	Retired	DNS, gearbox failed on warm-up lap
Kyalami	13	15	Two pit stops, vibration; finished 3 laps down
Jarama	6	Retired	Gearbox
Monte Carlo	6	6	Four pit stops, goggles; finished 3 laps down
Nivelles	13	6	Fuel stop; finished 1 lap down
Clermont Ferrand	1	3	Pit stop, puncture
Brands Hatch	17	4	Finished 1 lap down
Nürburgring	8	15	Started from pits; finished 1 lap down
Österreichring	6	5	
Monza	2	Retired	Brakes, worn pads
Mosport Park	10	6	Finished 1 lap down
Watkins Glen	7	15	Started from back; finished 2 laps down
Zolder	15	6	Finished 3 laps down
Monte Carlo	12	Retired	Overheating
Silverstone	29	Retired	Fuel pressure
Zandvoort	18	Retired	Fuel pressure
Österreichring	DNS	Retired	DNS, no engine
Mosport Park	11	10	Pit stop, tyres; finished 3 laps down
Watkins Glen	12	Retired	DNS, withdrew after Cevert's death
Jarama	23	Retired	Brake shaft failure

Date	Team	Car-Engine	Tyres
26 May	Chris Amon Racing	3.0 Amon AF101-Cosworth V8	F
4 August	Chris Amon Racing	3.0 Amon AF101-Cosworth V8	F
8 September	Chris Amon Racing	3.0 Amon AF101-Cosworth V8	F
22 September	British Racing Motors	3.0 BRM P201 V12	F
6 October	British Racing Motors	3.0 BRM P201 V12	F

1975

17 August	HB Bewaking Team Ensign	3.0 Ensign N175-Cosworth V8	G
7 September	HB Bewaking Team Ensign	3.0 Ensign N175-Cosworth V8	G

1976

6 March	Team Ensign	3.0 Ensign N174-Cosworth V8	G
28 March	Team Ensign	3.0 Ensign N174-Cosworth V8	G
2 May	Team Ensign	3.0 Ensign N176-Cosworth V8	G
16 May	Team Ensign	3.0 Ensign N176-Cosworth V8	G
30 May	Team Ensign	3.0 Ensign N176-Cosworth V8	G
13 June	Team Ensign	3.0 Ensign N176-Cosworth V8	G
18 July	Team Ensign	3.0 Ensign N176-Cosworth V8	G
1 August	Team Ensign	3.0 Ensign N176-Cosworth V8	G
3 October	Walter Wolf Racing	3.0 Williams FW05-Cosworth V8	G

Circuit	Qualified	Finished	Race Report
Monte Carlo	20	Retired	Hub failure
Nürburgring	DNQ	DNQ	Unwell
Monza	DNQ	Retired	DNQ
Mosport Park	25	Retired	Pit stop, misfire; finished 10 laps down
Watkins Glen	12	9	Finished 2 laps down
Österreichring	23	12	Finished 1 lap down
Monza	19	12	Misfire; finished 4 laps down
Kyalami	18	14	Pit stop, fuel; finished 2 laps down
Long Beach	17	8	Pit stop, brakes; finished 2 laps down
Jarama	10	5	Finished 1 lap down
Zolder	8	Retired	Lost wheel, crashed
Monte Carlo	13	13	Painful wrist; finished 4 laps down
Anderstorp	3	Retired	Suspension failure, crashed
Brands Hatch	6	Retired	Water leak
Nürburgring	17	Retired	Withdrew
Mosport Park	DNS	Retired:	DNS, practice accident